A Devotional Journey into the Mass

CHRISTOPHER CARSTENS

A DEVOTIONAL JOURNEY

INTO THE

MASS

How Mass Can Become a Time of
Grace, Nourishment, and Devotion

Edited with a foreword by Dan Burke

SPIRITUAL DIRECTION
SERIES

SOPHIA INSTITUTE PRESS

Manchester, New Hampshire

Sophia Institute Press
Box 5284, Manchester, NH 03108
1-800-888-9344
www.SophiaInstitute.com

Sophia Institute Press® is a registered trademark of Sophia Institute.

Library of Congress Cataloging-in-Publication Data

Names: Carstens, Christopher, 1970- author.
Title: A devotional journey into the Mass : how Mass can become a time of grace, nourishment, and devotion / Christopher Carstens ; edited with a foreword by Dan Burke.
Description: Manchester, New Hampshire : Sophia Institute Press, 2018. | Series: Spiritual direction series | Includes bibliographical references.
Identifiers: LCCN 2017049140 | ISBN 9781622824809 (pbk. : alk. paper)
Subjects: LCSH: Mass.
Classification: LCC BX2230.3 .C37 2018 | DDC 264/.02036—dc23 LC record available at https://lccn.loc.gov/2017049140

Second printing

Contents

FOREWORD

Signposts in a Strange Land

✠

Sacred Signs by twentieth-century Catholic thinker and pioneer of liturgical reform Romano Guardini has haunted me since my first reading. The writer's luminous insights about what it means to enter into and participate in the sacred feast of the Mass are without compare and worthy of anyone who desires to deepen his union with the Blessed Trinity in and through the Mass.

The liturgical participation Guardini has in mind engages sensible signs, since the liturgy, he writes, is "sacramental in its nature." The method of his 1917 book is "to study those actions that are still in present day use, those visible signs which believers have received and made their own and use to express the 'invisible grace.' . . . We need to be shown how, or by some means incited, to see and feel and make the sacred signs ourselves."[1] Even so, Guardini's reflections are very brief and written at a time when many more things were taken for granted than can be today.

My desire in commissioning Christopher Carstens to write *A Devotional Journey into the Mass* is tied to Guardini. I wanted a book that would resurrect Guardini's sacramental approach

---

[1] Romano Guardini, *Sacred Signs*, introduction.

to active participation in a way that would address our present, post–Vatican II context, so that a new generation of the faithful could enjoy the same benefit.

The disastrous liturgical confusion following the Second Vatican Council led to a lack of focus on the importance of the faithful's full, active, and conscious participation in the Mass, at least as was intended by the Council. This book is meant to make up for what is lacking in the faithful's understanding of authentic liturgical participation and to help clarify the authentic intent and wisdom of the Council while mirroring, as much as possible, Guardini's powerful devotional tone. The end result, we hope, is that any layperson or cleric who reads this work, regardless of background or formation concerning the Mass, will find a beautiful path into the unfathomable beauty of the Holy Sacrifice of the Mass.

But the Mass isn't magic, and its signs cannot engage us against our will. As we seek to enter more deeply into the Church's greatest liturgical mystery and to participate more fully in its saving work, we must understand that our cooperation is essential. To that end, before even turning to the first page of Carstens's work, let us keep a few important questions in mind:

+ What is it that we want from God in the Mass?

+ What is it that He wants from us?

+ How can we encounter Him in the Mass in a way that refreshes our souls and draws us ever more deeply into His presence?

+ Are there ways in which we can better prepare ourselves for this life-changing encounter?

The good news is that each of these questions has a rich and rewarding answer, but it will require some work on our part to discover how rich and how rewarding. To help us in this discovery, we must first see that central to any understanding of the Mass is the idea of *mystagogy*—the process whereby we are led from the sacred signs of the liturgy to the heavenly realities they contain. This is the approach Carstens takes in inviting us to read and live out what he reveals in this book.

As we enter into this reality of the mystery we explore, our intellect is an aid—but only an aid. What we enter into is truth, but "truth as Person"—the experience of Jesus in our time and place, as Pope Benedict XVI reflected. Entering into the mystery is an adventure of encounter, of coming before and entering into the heart of God. This encounter takes us beyond the limitations of our intellect into the living Person of Christ at the heart of the Mass.

Needless to say, any encounter with Christ in the Mass cannot be facilitated by a cursory reading of Carstens's work, a quick jaunt that misses the finer details of the Mass. Nor will we find it fruitful to undertake an arid reading of this work, one that engages the mind but ignores the heart. Instead we must follow *A Devotional Journey into the Mass* as a prayer, as an expressed desire, as a request to and for God, with an openness to His self-revelation. We would do well to aid in this adventure by reading this book in a setting conducive to prayer, such as in an adoration chapel or with a prayer group. Whatever our approach, this book will inevitably guide us to a place where our appreciation and experience of the Lord in the Mass is far richer and more lasting in impact than we may have thought possible. The truth can change our lives. That notion has been a guiding principle in this project—for both Carstens and myself. And that's the beautiful thing about the truth's transformative power. When a prayerful, open heart encounters the truth, it also encounters the One who is the Way, the Truth, and the Life.

— Dan Burke

Introduction

———————✠———————

Laurence, my four-year-old son, when asked what he most liked about going to Mass, responded: "Eating donuts after." His sister seconded that response. While not the best of reasons, I guess it's a start.

But for many—including myself at one phase in my life—the reasons for going to Mass don't get much loftier. And while the Holy Spirit can and does use any number of reasons to call us to worship, if Laurence is still invoking donuts when he is fourteen, he probably won't be going to Mass when he is twenty-four. What do I, his father, need to show him about Mass in these, his formative years? How can I model for him a way of participating that motivates and maturates him? When he is twenty-four and asked about why he goes to Mass, I want him not to respond "donuts" but "divinization."

This book is written for Laurence and anyone who has ever wondered why he should participate in the Mass—and pondered how to do it. If I am going to spend an hour on Sunday at Mass, how can my participation make it an indispensable time of grace, nourishment, and devotion?

In the first major writing of his pontificate, Pope St. Pius X introduced the term "active participation" on behalf of the Magisterium. On November 22, 1903, the feast of St. Cecilia, he called for all members of the liturgical assembly to "active participation in the most holy mysteries and in the public and solemn prayer of the Church."[2] Why? The solemn prayer of the Church, that is, the liturgy, is the source of sanctity for all.

It is suggested that Pius X died with a heavy heart. This "parish priest of Christendom" witnessed not sanctity—at least not to the degree he hoped—but war. Pope Pius X died on August 20, 1914: less than two months after the assassination of Austrian Archduke Franz Ferdinand and only one month after the start of World War I. The combatants were nearly all Christians and, in the Church's view, should have acted differently, having had access to the liturgical font of holiness.

But Pius X's pastoral heart continued to beat throughout the Church, gaining strength for sixty years. On the same great feast of St. Cecilia, November 22, the Fathers of the Second Vatican Council approved the text of the Constitution on the Sacred Liturgy, *Sacrosanctum Concilium*. Promulgated officially by Blessed Pope Paul VI on December 4, 1963, the Council made "active participation" its leading liturgical litmus:

> Mother Church earnestly desires that all the faithful should be led to that fully conscious and active participation in liturgical celebrations which is demanded by the very nature of the liturgy. Such participation by the Christian people as "a chosen race, a royal priesthood, a

---

[2] Pius X, Motu Proprio *Tra Le Sollecitudini* (On Sacred Music), November 22, 1903.

holy nation, a redeemed people" (1 Pet. 2:9; cf. 2:4–5), is their right and duty by reason of their baptism.

In the restoration and promotion of the sacred liturgy, this full and active participation by all the people is the aim to be considered before all else; for it is the primary and indispensable source from which the faithful are to derive the true Christian spirit; and therefore pastors of souls must zealously strive to achieve it, by means of the necessary instruction, in all their pastoral work. (14)

But the triumph for "active participation" was not all that it appeared to be.

"Unfortunately," writes another liturgically minded pope, "the word [participation] was very quickly misunderstood to mean something external, entailing a need for general activity, as if as many people as possible, as often as possible, should be visibly engaged in action."[3] But if "active participation" is *not* principally an external and visible action, then what is it?

This book attempts to answer that question, giving eight simple ways to engage physically and spiritually, body and soul, in the saving work of Jesus Christ made present in the Mass. These eight reflections emanate from three foundational concerns:

1. The spiritual meaning of eight elements of the Mass

2. How we can fully, actively, and consciously participate in them

3. How our participation ought to affect our life in the world outside of Mass

---

[3] Joseph Ratzinger, *The Spirit of the Liturgy* (San Francisco: Ignatius Press, 2000), 171.

In the chapter "How to Listen to the Readings," for example, we will consider the Church's teaching that the Liturgy of the Word is a "dialogue between God and his people taking place through the Holy Spirit,"[4] a sort of microcosm of the larger dialogue between God and His people in the economy of salvation. Next, we will want to know how to participate in this divine dialogue: How can I take the word of God to heart and prepare a worthy response? Last, we will review some practical ways offered by the Church and her saints to prepare for the Liturgy of the Word's dialogue and how to keep it resounding in our ears during the week ahead (e.g., through *lectio divina*).

"Sacramentality" and, closely related to it, "mystagogy" will be the book's interpretive keys. While much can be gained in liturgical understanding by a study of liturgical law, history, documentation, pastoral practice, and so forth, the liturgy is first and foremost a *sacramental* reality. As the Constitution on the Sacred Liturgy says, "the liturgy is considered as an exercise of the priestly office of Jesus Christ," and this priestly work "is signified by signs perceptible to the senses, and is effected in a way which corresponds with each of these signs" (8).

The Jesus who carried out the Paschal Mystery in the flesh two thousand years ago is the same Jesus acting today in the sacraments. To touch, see, and hear Jesus today is to do so through the medium of the sacraments. It is the process of mystagogical catechesis that leads our natural senses to encounter the supernatural and liturgical Jesus. Thus, in focusing on each of these eight elements of the Mass, we focus on the signs and the symbols, the words and the actions of the Mass, each of which

---

[4] *Introduction to the Lectionary*, 28.

brings Christ and His saving work to the surface—so that we can actively participate with Him in His work.

In addition to sacramentality and mystagogy, other essential liturgical themes, including silence, Scripture, sacrifice, and priesthood, are incorporated into the chapters. The chapter "How to Prepare the Heart at the Offertory" focuses on the nature of sacrifice; "How to Pray the Opening Prayer" considers silence and reflection; and "How to Respond to the Dismissal" examines the life of holiness made available to us from liturgical participation.

Each of the baptized, says the Council, has not only a "right" but also a "duty" to participate actively. Jesus doesn't need our help in redeeming the world—but He wants it. Even though He is the liturgy's principal worker, He calls us to be His co-workers, His cooperators, His co-laborers (that is, His collaborators).

May the wisdom of the popes, the twentieth-century liturgical movement, and the teaching of the Second Vatican Council assist us in joining with Jesus Christ for His glory, our salvation, and the sanctification of the world.

1

How to Enter the
Church Building

✠

I am the door.

—John 10:9

Stand in front of your parish church, facing its main entrance. Or, if you can't do this at the moment, imagine — with as much detail as possible — that you are before it. What do you see?

While a church's face is as unique as any human face (are any two the same?), the ecclesial edifice usually shares characteristics with other sacred facades. A church's face announces its importance by greater ornamentation, such as windows, or unique moldings, or stone, brick, or other materials not seen on other parts of the building. Beautiful light fixtures adorn my parish's little church, and a Celtic cross sits atop the main entrance — Irish immigrants built the parish. The bell tower, if the church has one, is usually incorporated into the structure. A vestibule at the entrance gathers individuals from the street and ushers them into the nave, assembling them for worship.

But before all these other details, the door presents the key feature of the church's face. This holy door is often elevated, accessible only by ascending steps. Like the larger structure that houses it, the materials used in the door's construction are often of higher quality and craftsmanship than those of other doors. Even the size of the door — it is probably the largest one in the church — shows its importance. And this door has ushers and greeters (formerly called "porters") who minister to it and those who pass through it.

As an artist drawing a human face would include eyes, ears, nose, mouth, and chin in his sketch, so you see before you in your own church's "face" towers, windows, doors, and doormen — the details we all expect a church to include. But more than a merely human face, through craftsmanship, elevation, size, and beauty, each element of a church is designed to reflect and draw our hearts to heavenly realities.

Although not every church entrance is as beautiful as another — nor is every painted portrait a Madonna — still, a church's entrance says something to the pilgrim about to enter, something different from the other sides of the church, and something different, say, from the face of a Walmart, a Walgreens, or a Wendy's.

When I asked you to imagine your parish church, were you uncertain where to look?

It is a truth of our nature that men and women come to know reality, as well as make themselves known, through the medium of sensible signs and symbols that can be seen, touched, tasted, smelled, or heard. You know the thoughts of my mind through the letters, words, and sentences seen on this page. I know that my son Laurence is playing outside while I write this because I can hear his voice. Through symbols, too, we know the difference between an image of St. Peter and one of St. Paul — the first holds a set of keys, and the second bears a sword. Even when our physical senses seem to be sleeping, our minds are filling up with images in our dreams.

This distinctly human feature—the ability to create and comprehend symbols—is also an especially Catholic one. Called the "sacramental principle," it means that the invisible God communicates with us through sensible signs. But our Lord's "sacramental communication" isn't simply of knowledge alone but of His very life. God touches our whole being through sacramental things.

Even a cursory glance at the Gospels shows us that Jesus speaks of Himself in sacramental terms. For example, when the apostle Philip asks Jesus to show the Apostles the Father, Jesus replies: "Have I been with you for so long a time, and you still do not know me, Philip? Whoever has seen me has seen the Father" (John 14:9). Furthermore, the Letter to the Hebrews recognizes this same sacramental element in the Savior, calling Jesus the radiance of God's glory and "the very imprint of his being" (Heb. 1:3). In both passages, the incarnate Christ appears a visible, audible, touchable man, who is, at the same time, the bearer of the unseen Father. Earlier I asked you to "imagine" your parish church, to use images that present the absent building to your mind, before your eyes. So, too, Jesus is "the *image* of the invisible God" (Col. 1:15). St. Augustine would say simply, "There is no other mystery [i.e., sacrament] of God, except Christ" (see *Catechism of the Catholic Church* [CCC] 774).

Like Jesus, the Church has a sacramental quality about her. Invoking the first Adam, from whom God had drawn Eve, the Second Vatican Council says poetically that "it was from the side of Christ as he slept the sleep of death upon the cross that there came forth 'the wondrous sacrament of the whole

Church.'"[5] More directly, the same Council teaches that "it is of the essence of the Church that she be both human and divine, visible yet invisibly equipped, eager to act and yet intent on contemplation, present in this world and yet not at home in it."[6] To see the Church feed the poor is to see Christ. To hear the Church proclaim the Good News is to hear Christ. To offer our prayers on her altar is to join ourselves to the sacrifice of Christ. In all of her sensible activities, she makes the otherwise unseen Jesus present in our midst.

When most of us hear the word "sacrament," we quickly think of the seven, those "outward signs, instituted by Christ, to give grace." Like Jesus, who is their content, and the Church, who is their guardian, these seven ritual signs are the privileged places where we encounter Christ today. Jesus has ascended into heaven but has not ceased working for us. On the contrary, "Christ now lives and acts in and with his Church, in a new way appropriate to this new age. He acts through the sacraments" (CCC 1076). The Jesus who forgave sins, breathed the Holy Spirit upon the apostles, and fed His apostles with His Body and Blood is the same Jesus who does these actions for us today. What He once did in the flesh, He now does through the sacraments. Jesus is the same; His work is the same: only the medium is different. "What was visible in our Savior," St. Leo the Great explains, "has passed over into his mysteries [i.e., sacraments]" (see CCC 1115).

As Catholics we see that same Savior at least every Sunday at Mass—but not only in the Blessed Sacrament. As important as

---

[5] Second Vatican Council, Constitution on the Sacred Liturgy *Sacrosanctum Concilium*, December 4, 1963, no. 5.

[6] Ibid., no. 2.

the sacraments are, there are other signs and symbols that make up the liturgy, and each of these has a sacramental quality about it, such that Jesus can be encountered in them as well. Ashes, palms, Paschal candles, and holy water are sacramentals that resemble the sacraments because they communicate grace through outward signs. Beyond these sacramentals are other liturgical elements that, in some way, are epiphanies of Christ: stained-glass windows, the priest's chair, the sung "Holy, holy, holy," the people's response "And with your spirit," Sunday (that first day of the week), bowing, the book of the Gospels, the assembly, and — to bring us face-to-face with our parish church again — the church door. While these sacramental elements don't equal the Blessed Sacrament in their efficacy, nevertheless, they remain potential encounters with Jesus.

Here is the essential point: sacraments and sacramental signs and symbols are filled with Jesus. They are the favored "face" of Jesus in today's world. More than mere mental reminders, and more effective than simple pointers that direct us elsewhere, liturgical sacraments and sacramentals unite heaven and earth. If you have ever seen Michelangelo's fresco *The Creation of Adam* adorning the ceiling of the Sistine Chapel, you may recall that both God and Adam are reaching toward each other, but their fingers are not touching. Sin makes that distance between them a chasm, but Jesus bridges the divide. Liturgical signs and symbols, filled with Christ, connect us with God. Awareness of this "sacramental principle" is the first step on a devotional journey into the Mass, and a key concept in actively participating in the Mass as the Church intends. So, let us now return to where we began: standing before our parish church.

What should enter our minds as we enter our Church's door? In a word, Jesus. He Himself says: "I am the door. Whoever enters through me will be saved, and will come in and go out and find pasture" (John 10:9). "Door" is a strange name for a person. (Try calling your spouse or child or co-worker that and see how he or she reacts.) Although Jesus isn't *literally* a door, He is the only way to enter paradise. And this door to paradise was not always open.

There was another door our first parents had to contend with —which until Christ's coming served more as a wall than a portal—and the history of salvation is written on this seemingly merciless wall. First, following Adam and Eve's Original Sin, God expelled them, "stationing the cherubim and the fiery revolving sword east of the garden of Eden, to guard the way to the tree of life" (Gen. 3:24). The gate between heaven and earth closed—only to be reopened by the oiling of its frozen hinges by the Anointed One.

Yet we don't have to wait for the Annunciation to see this saving gate, since we can see this future "door" opening Himself at the moment of the Chosen People's exodus from Egypt's slavery. Part of God's instructions to the Israelites for this first Passover meal included taking some of the blood of the unblemished lamb and smearing it on "the two doorposts and the lintel of the houses in which they eat it." God continues, "The blood will mark the houses where you are. Seeing the blood, I will pass over you; thereby, when I strike the land of Egypt, no destructive blow will come upon you" (Exod.12:7, 13). Here, the door signifies belonging to God, protection from death, and serves as the initial portal on the journey to the Promised Land.

Five hundred years later, the first Temple of Solomon is built in Jerusalem atop Mount Moriah. Its own gates—just as the Temple itself—anticipate Christ and the opening path to eternal life. Jerusalem was God's city, and the Temple formed its heart—the place of sacrifice and of becoming one with God. To climb Mount Moriah, and enter the Holy City, and worship at the Temple was to return to God and the communion once lived with Him in the Garden. In fact, even the Temple itself was decorated with images of trees, plants, deer, water, and fruit. So the Chosen People prayed: "I rejoiced when I heard them say: 'Let us go to God's house.' And now our feet are standing within your gates, O Jerusalem" (Ps. 122:1–2). And again, "Open to me the gates of holiness: I will enter and give thanks. This is the LORD's own gate where the just may enter" (Ps. 118:19–20). The gates into these sacred places were no mere practical passageways but thresholds to heaven. Sound familiar? If you're still imagining your parish church, this description should ring a bell—or at least open some doors for you.

The New Temple, the temple of Christ's body (see John 2:21), is the heavenly Jerusalem. As St. John relates, "I saw no temple in the city, for its temple is the Lord God almighty and the Lamb" (Rev. 21:22). Can you imagine the gates into such a city? We don't need to: the Holy City of Jerusalem "had a massive, high wall, with twelve gates where twelve angels were stationed and on which names were inscribed, [the names] of the twelve tribes of the Israelites.... The twelve gates were twelve pearls, each of the gates made from a single pearl" (Rev. 21:12, 21). These "pearly gates" announce the heavenly homeland, just as our churches and their doors are "signs and symbols of heavenly realities."[7]

So the door to the parish church, which stands before us now—physically or in our minds—is no ordinary entrance. It

---

[7] Second Vatican Council, *Sacrosanctum Concilium* 122.

appears different because it *is* different: it is a mark of God's house and a sign protecting those within, as at that first Passover. It is an entrance into the Great King's city and His Temple—whose curtain is now torn open—where we touch God, as in Jerusalem. It is a sign of a new heavens and a new earth, where we eat from the "tree of life that is in the garden of God" (Rev. 2:7), as in heaven. If this door had a name, it would be "Jesus," for He is our identification, our salvation, our Passover, our communion, our eternal life.

In our journey into the heart of the Mass, we must start off on the right foot. As we approach the main entrance (don't go in the side door!), pause for a moment and consider that we approach Christ the Door, our access to the Father. Jesus stands at the door and knocks (Rev. 3:20), awaiting our entry. Let us "go within his gates, giving thanks," and "enter his courts with songs of praise" (see Ps. 100:4).

Not all eyes see the church's door in this light, nor all feet pass through gladly and with determination. But the "sacramental principle"—that the unseen God comes to us, and we go to Him, through sensible signs—assists us in actively and intelligently participating in the Mass. Jesus said it would take real insight to see Him, even as a door: "How narrow the gate and constricted the road that leads to life. And those who find it are few" (Matt. 7:14).

Seeing the "sacramental principle" is the first step in getting to the heart of the Mass. In our next chapter, we will acquire the Church's perception and experience how the outward sign—the door, for example—can draw us into the spiritual reality.

In Brief

+ The "sacramental principle" means that the invisible God communicates with us through sensible signs.

+ Jesus, "the image of the invisible God," is likened to a sacrament of God the Father, since He makes the Father present and accessible.

+ The Church, like a sacrament, is an outward and visible sign of Jesus, whose body she is.

+ The Church's seven sacraments and her sacramentals communicate "Christ-life" to us by means of external symbols.

+ Each element of the liturgy has a sacramental quality about it and is a potential grace-filled encounter with Jesus.

+ Our active and devout participation encounters Jesus in all things liturgical: God is in the details!

THE NEXT TIME YOU GO TO MASS

✦ Enter through the main door of the church with a prayer, in your own words, to Jesus the Door.

✦ Recall the "sacramental principle," knowing that each element of the liturgy is meant to bring us to a real encounter with Jesus.

✦ Pay attention! The miracle at the Wedding Feast of Cana happened because Mary *noticed* that the couple was out of wine. See with spiritual insight and hear with supernatural hearing the many elements that come together at Mass.

2

How to Make the Sign of the Cross

The Lord God made grow every tree that was delightful to look at and good for food, with the tree of life in the middle of the garden.

—Genesis 2:9

Estimates vary, but most of the population falls short of 20/20 vision, the standard for perfect sight. To correct our visual short-comings, modern medicine offers a multitude of solutions, from eyeglasses to contacts, from laser to cataract surgery, from anti-allergens to glaucoma drops. Each treatment, if successful, helps us to see what is there.

Vision, like the rest of our senses, connects us to reality, and when our eyes fail, we risk losing our contact with the natural world. We may *not* see things that are there—that last step on the staircase, the oncoming car, or this little book. More troubling than losing our physical sight, though, is losing our mental sight. Should our minds begin to fail, we might *start* seeing things that really *aren't* there—while I hope to resemble Pope St. John Paul II and his love for the liturgy, if I literally see myself as Pope John Paul II, I am delusional.

What is true for our natural senses is just as correct for our supernatural perception. If our supernatural vision suffers from defects in our development, or from a cloudy intellect, or from the darkness of sin, or from spiritual shortsightedness, we cannot hope to see clearly what (or who) is before us. And, as we saw in the last chapter, the reality of the liturgical life is none other than Jesus Himself, made present to us in sacramental signs. Mother Nature intends us to have 20/20 vision so that we can see and love the natural world; Mother Church wants us to see with equal clarity Jesus, so that we can experience fullness of life with Him in the supernatural world.

As our eye doctor offers glasses and drops to correct our natural vision, the Church provides her own prescription for bringing the Mass's truths into focus. After all, as we discussed in the last chapter, which of us saw our parish's main door as Jesus? I had walked through church doors many times before it ever crossed my mind that I could be encountering Jesus as I crossed the church threshold (and, truth be told, I don't always see "Christ the door" now). Whether we're discussing doors to churches or windows to our souls—our eyes—the Church's remedy for our liturgical shortsightedness is called "mystagogical catechesis."

Don't be frightened by the name—what it describes is not as intimidating as it sounds. Recall that each element of the Mass has a sacramental quality, where the otherwise unseen Jesus is made present before us through sensible signs—what we called the sacramental principle. The doors in the church's edifice and the Eucharist on the church's altar, although they differ in some ways (in their institution, for example), resemble each other insofar as their reality (Jesus) and their medium (signs) are the same. Mystagogical catechesis (or simply "mystagogy") leads us, the perceivers, from the outward sign (e.g., door or bread) to an encounter with the inward reality, Jesus. The *Catechism of the Catholic Church*, which naturally offers mystagogical catechesis, explains the vision this way: "Liturgical catechesis aims to initiate people into the mystery of Christ (It is 'mystagogy.') by proceeding from the visible to the invisible, from the sign to the thing signified, from the 'sacraments' to the 'mysteries'" (1075). When I see the door, I ought to see Jesus. When I hear the "Holy, holy, holy," I must hear the choirs of angels around Jesus' throne. When I make the Sign of the Cross—our topic for this chapter—I want to encounter Jesus' Cross. If I don't perceive Jesus in the church's doors, songs, and crosses, I am not seeing what is there: my vision is not 20/20. Like the Pharisees, who were face-to-face with Jesus, I would "have eyes and not see, ears and not hear" (Mark 8:18).

How does mystagogy serve as a sort of "liturgical lasik surgery"? How can it lead me into and through the sacramental signs to a real encounter with Jesus himself? It does so, first, by uncovering the meaning of the Mass's sacramental signs and symbols, and also by showing how they are connected to Christ. As the *Catechism* explains, "A sacramental celebration is woven from signs and symbols. In keeping with the divine pedagogy of salvation, their meaning is rooted in the work of creation and in human culture, specified by the events of the Old Covenant and fully revealed in the person and work of Christ." Additionally, many sacramental signs and symbols "prefigure and anticipate the glory of heaven" (1145, 1152).

The word "rooted" in the *Catechism*'s description is especially helpful to our discussion of mystagogy. Think of an apple, for instance. To find out how and why the apple tastes the way it does, you would have to look to the roots of the tree. What is the tree's soil like: rich? rocky? sandy? Most likely, it's a stratified soil with different layers of earth, each rich in its own nutrients. You would also need to know the kind of atmospheric conditions that accompanied the fruit's growth, such as the moisture, temperature, and sunlight. When considering how to produce the best apple crop, a farmer takes all these elements into account, or tries to, and plants a seed most conducive to the conditions, so that his fruit will be the best possible.

Others have thought of sacraments in horticultural terms as well. For instance, St. Albert the Great (d. 1280) once likened the Eucharist to the fruit of the Tree of the Cross. And if we wanted to know how the Eucharist is the substantial presence of Jesus, we would, like the *Catechism* and the successful farmer, consider the roots from which the Blessed Sacrament "grew." These roots extend into a soil that, at its deepest level, is made of creation and nature. Immediately above it is a second layer consisting of human culture and social life. A third level consists of the figures, people, and events of the Old Testament, those that anticipate Jesus' saving work. And it is Jesus—His life, teaching, and actions—that constitutes the tree's topsoil, the most fertile for the tree's fruit. The heavenly rain that waters the tree and the noonday sun that energizes its growth are the fifth source of meaning for the Eucharist. These five fonts of meaning—(1) creation, (2) human nature, (3) the Old Testament, (4) the life of Jesus, and (5) heaven—fill the Mass's signs and symbols with substantial meaning. To know these sources—which is what mystagogy helps us discover—is to see behind these symbols to the reality of a person: Jesus.

In the first chapter, we took a mystagogical look at the door of the local parish church. To claim that this portal of wood and glass is Jesus is one thing (as He Himself had claimed); but to show *how* it is Jesus, we looked back to the door that closed on the Garden after creation and its fall and to the door of the Israelites' houses in Egypt and in Jerusalem, and we looked forward to the pearly doors in heaven's gates. By looking at the church door through these sacramental and mystagogical lenses, we saw it for what it was—more than a mere passage into the building, but an encounter with Salvation's own Gate.

Now that our liturgical eye exam is complete, and a prescription has been given to help improve our supernatural perception, we can continue our journey into the Mass with eyes wide open. After we've passed through the doors into the church, the first thing we usually do when we enter is make the Sign of the Cross—and it is to this common yet symbolically laden ritual that we turn our attention next—mystagogically, of course.

It is a common practice to dip our fingers into the holy-water stoup near the door of the church and make the Sign of the Cross. We then continue to our pew and pray privately, beginning and ending with the Sign of the Cross. As Mass starts, the priest and all present sign themselves with the Sign of the Cross. But why? What does this sign mean? And how has it come to mean what it means?

We notice from the outset that making the Sign of the Cross consists in both words—"In the name of the Father, and of the Son, and of the Holy Spirit"—and in the action of moving the right hand from forehead to the chest, then from the left shoulder to the right. Words and gestures are regularly found together in the Mass's signs. "A sacramental celebration," says the *Catechism*, "is a meeting of God's children with their Father, in Christ and the Holy Spirit; this meeting takes the form of a dialogue, through actions and words" (1153). We can consider each part of the Sign of the Cross, the words and the action, according to their roots and see how there is more to the Sign of the Cross than initially meets the eye.

Following the five-step mystogical process described above, the believer trying to understand the Sign of the Cross first looks for meaning in creation. In this realm, we observe both a Trinity of persons and a life-giving tree. The Trinity is named at creation, even if subtly, as the scriptural account of the creation of the world attests. The first verses of the first chapter of the Bible's first book say: "In the beginning when God created the heavens and the earth, the earth was a formless void and darkness covered the face of the deep, while a wind from God swept over the face of the waters. Then God said, 'Let there be light'; and there was light" (Gen. 1:1–3, NRSV). We notice God the Father, who creates "heaven and earth," God the Holy Spirit, a wind, or breath of God over the waters, and God the Son, the Word, through whom the Father speaks, "Let there be light."

In addition to the presence of Father, Son, and Holy Spirit at the moment of creation, a tree also grows in the creation account, not unlike the one we trace upon our bodies while calling upon the Blessed Trinity. "Out of the ground the Lord God made grow every tree that was delightful to look at and good for food, with the tree of life in the middle of the garden and the tree of the knowledge of good and evil" (Gen. 2:9). We read later that it was only the fruit from the tree of the knowledge of good and evil that shouldn't be eaten, but that the tree of life could sustain their lives (Gen. 2:16–17). Another "tree of life," the Cross of Jesus, would later bear fruit for a new creation.

If we recall this first creation account when making the Sign of the Cross, we should see in the Mass's first words and actions the persons of the Trinity, who made us from the heart of Their being. We can unite ourselves with all of creation, which till now has been "groaning in labor pains" (Rom. 8:22), as God's new creation begins. The tree of life, rejected by Adam and Eve, marks our bodies and feeds our souls.

Human nature and the social lives of men and women throughout the ages provide a second category of sacramental meaning for the Sign of the Cross. Consider where the bounty is found in Robert Louis Stevenson's *Treasure Island*: on the X that marks the spot on Long John Silver's map. To "be at a crossroads" signifies an important decision, while "being crossed" means conflict. We can plot points on the x and y axes of a graph — itself the shape of a cross — to represent facts in the real world. Here, human culture — whether Catholic or not — finds in the cross treasure, importance, conflict, and reality. At Mass, "the Church presupposes, integrates and sanctifies elements from creation and human culture, conferring on them the dignity of signs of grace, of the new creation in Jesus Christ" (CCC 1149). Our Sign of the Cross becomes more meaningful the more mystagogically deeper we look.

While it might seem strange to claim that we find meaning in a pre-Christian source for a supremely Catholic custom, the Old Testament yields our third source of meaning for the Sign of the Cross. If we imagine the Old Testament as a layer of nourishing soil feeding the roots of the great tree of life, the crosses it contains become more substantial as we approach the topsoil of this fertile ground. A first cross appears in the blessing of Jacob's grandsons, Manasseh and Ephraim. It was customary, as it is today, to extend a blessing (or a greeting, as in a handshake) with the right hand. Manasseh, the elder brother, was entitled to the larger blessing through the right hand, while Ephraim, the younger, would receive his part through the left (or, in Latin, the *sinister*) hand. Accordingly, the boys' father, Joseph, "took the two, Ephraim with his right hand, to Israel's [i.e., Jacob's] left, and Manasseh with his left hand, to Israel's right, and brought them up to him. But Israel, crossing his hands, put out his right hand and laid it on the head of Ephraim, although he was the younger, and his left hand on the head of Manasseh, although he was the firstborn" (Gen. 48:13–14). This X made with Jacob's arms while blessing his grandchildren (imagine yourself doing as Jacob had done), foreshadows Jesus and His Cross, the source of all blessing. Further loading Jacob's action with meaning, the X is also the Greek letter *chi*, the first letter of Christ's name in Greek, Χρῆστος.

Another Old Testament cross is seen in the person of Moses, traditionally interpreted as an image of the Christ to come. Along their journey to the Promised Land, the Chosen People engage in battle with the Amalekites. Moses, interceding for the Israelites from atop a nearby hill, raised his hands, forming a cross with his limbs, trunk and head. "As long as Moses kept his hands raised up, Israel had the better of the fight, but when he let his hands rest, Amalek had the better of the fight" (Exod. 17:11). So necessary was the cross-shaped-Moses for victory that two assistants propped up his arms when he grew tired!

The Old Testament includes other prefigurements of the Cross, but these two examples show us what the Sign of the Cross means as Mass begins: all blessings reach us through the Cross of Christ, and beneath its sign we will travel victorious on our exodus from this life into the promised land of heaven.

The *Catechism* says plainly that in the Mass, Jesus "is the meaning of all these signs" (1151). By this we are to understand that Jesus fills each sacramental sign with Himself and gives each sign its true meaning. When we trace the Sign of the Cross over our bodies, we trace its meaning to His own saving Cross atop Mount Calvary. His Cross—and now ours—is the tree of life, history's "X marks the spot" and our own life's "crossroads," our source of blessing and our weapon against sin. But the words we say while crossing ourselves are also the words of the Word—Jesus our Lord. In the moments before His Ascension, Jesus commands His apostles to "go . . . and make disciples of all nations, baptizing them in the name of the Father, and of the Son, and of the holy Spirit" (Matt. 28:19). The Sign of the Cross, therefore, made with awareness and love, is not only an imitation of Jesus and His Cross, but the obedient response of the faithful to the final command our Lord makes in His earthly ministry.

As a sacramental sign's fifth source of meaning, heaven also shows the glory of the Cross. The prophet Ezekiel once had a vision that those citizens of Jerusalem marked with "an X on the foreheads" would not be slain in the punishment of the idolatrous (Ezek. 9:1–11). St. John, looking into the new Jerusalem, sees these same saved souls: "Do not damage the land or the sea or the trees until we put the seal on the foreheads of the servants of our God" (Rev. 7:3). The forehead's mark does not simply save those who bear it from destruction, but more positively gives them access once again to the heavenly tree of life: "To the victor I will give the right to eat from the tree of life that is in the garden of God" (Rev. 2:7). The Sign of the Cross not only looks backward to history's Cross of two thousand years ago but even now shares in heaven's tree of life and partakes of the divine food it yields.

Now that we've taken a full measure of the Cross's dimensions in history, mystery, and majesty, let's summarize what we see when we look at the Sign of the Cross through mystagogical glasses. In it we find our creation from the hands of the Trinity and, along with the entire cosmos, our new creation today. By this sign we are nourished with God-given grace, as from the very tree of life in nature's original garden. The Sign of the Cross channels Christ-life to us and, as the Chosen People on their way to a Promised Land experienced, the Cross is our standard and protection along life's pilgrimage. In the Sign of the Cross we configure ourselves to Jesus and His Cross, while responding from the heart to His command to teach and baptize. The Sign of the Cross we make every time we attend Mass also transports us to heaven, where, along with the victorious saints, we eat the fruit of the tree of life in a restored Garden. There is so much to experience in the Sign of the Cross — but only for those who have eyes to see and ears to hear.

A final note on the term "mystagogy" — which by now may not appear nearly as intimidating as it did when we started this chapter. This process whereby we are drawn into the things of heaven through earthly symbols is not some kind of decoder ring that cracks a secret message. Rather, it helps us to look to the roots of signs and symbols alive with Jesus — be these doors, crosses, or Trinitarian names — and to understand from where these visual aids for heaven were born. Knowing these origins will give us the start of our new birth unto eternal life with Jesus.

The Sign of the Cross, when made thoughtfully and lovingly, lifts us to heaven. In our next step into the heart of the Mass, we will listen — and *not* listen — to the Mass's Opening Prayer, where our intentions are collected by the Church and launched heavenward.

In Brief

+ Because Catholics celebrate a sacramental liturgy, our faith formation encourages a "mystagogical catechesis," which leads us from the outward part of the sacramental sign to its inward reality.

+ Perception that sees or hears only the outward action or word is missing what is truly and really present: Jesus.

+ Mystagogy leads the attentive participant from the visible to the invisible by uncovering the roots of sacramental meaning in creation, culture, the Old Testament, Christ, and heaven.

+ The Sign of the Cross, in its words and gesture, is an especially rich sign in the Mass. Like any tree in the natural world, this tree of life extends its root into multilayered soil—creation, human culture, the Old Testament, and the life and work of Jesus—while it is nourished from above by the "dew" of the Holy Spirit and the Sun of heaven.

THE NEXT TIME YOU GO TO MASS

+ Recall the birth and growth of the Sign of the Cross, the tree of life, from its many sources.

+ Make a Sign of the Cross that is large and not rushed.

+ Recall that your heart is at the center of the Sign of the Cross—at the crossbeams of the gesture, and surrounded by the Father, the Son, and the Holy Spirit.

+ Teach another person—a child, a spouse, a friend, a CCD student—the meaning and importance of the Sign of the Cross.

3

How to Pray the Opening Prayer

✠

They devoted themselves . . . to the prayers.

—Acts 2:42

Signposts make any journey easier, especially those trips to new and unfamiliar destinations. If it's my first time traveling to Timbuktu, I'll want to know where I can get fuel along the way, which way to turn en route, where I can find water and other essential road snacks—beef jerky, potato chips, and such—and the location of the next rest stop. I can find this information from road signs or my tried-and-true, if somewhat dog-eared, Rand McNally atlas, and even the Information Highway can help me on my real-time highway journey, thanks to Siri and Google Maps. Without these travel aids my trip risks becoming a dead end.

The same sort of preparation is necessary too—although in a more profoundly spiritual way—for our devotional journey into the Mass. How do I go deeper into the mystery of the Church's greatest prayer? Who are my companions on this journey? What stops will we need to make along the way? Where are the maps and legends, the signposts and traffic signals that will allow me to take my bearings on this journey into mystery?

We have seen already in our look at doors and crosses how Old Testament people and events reveal some of the meaning of what we do in the Mass. Here is another such occasion — and sign — that makes the Mass's landscape more navigable. Picture the Chosen People as they cross Sinai's desert, filled with serpents and scorpions. They have left Egypt's fleshpots but cannot yet see their destination. Manna from heaven satisfies their hunger, and water from the rock quenches their thirst. They follow their leader, Moses — sometimes grudgingly — as he follows the Column of Cloud and the Pillar of Fire. In the end, as salvation history tells us, the Chosen People reach a land flowing with milk and honey.

Faithful Catholics take a similar road trip during Mass. Its Opening Prayer keeps us pilgrims from wandering off into unchartered and dangerous territory. From the church's doors we began a voyage from a world of fleshpots, sin, darkness, and slavery, with all its fears and hopes, to the prelude of another world, a heavenly port to freedom and fulfillment such as the world of fleshpots and folly could never understand. God's own food and drink — the Eucharistic bread and wine — will nourish us along the way. The bishop, like Moses with staff in hand, or the priest in his stead, stands at the head of the assembled pilgrims and directs us. And the Opening Prayer, or Collect, appears as a key mile marker that bonds the Church's travelers, diverse in circumstance but united in our desire to reach a shared destination.

With voices joined into a single band, the faithful arrive at this first stop on the journey into mystery (the Introductory Rites) while we move onward, impelled into the heart of the Mass. But let's check our map for a moment. How should this pilgrim assembly pray the Opening Prayer in such a way that it guides us to the Promised Land—without all the detours and distractions followed by the stiff-necked (and probably stiff-backed and footsore) travelers among the Chosen People?

According to our map, which is the layout of the Mass, informed by tradition and catechesis, we will engage fruitfully in the Opening Prayer only when we first understand that these words our priest offers and the corresponding assent our hearts make at this point in the Mass is *prayer*. There are many descriptions of prayer, but St. Augustine offers an image that the desert-traveling Chosen People could appreciate, when he calls prayer "the encounter of God's thirst with ours. God thirsts that we may thirst for him" (CCC 2560).[8] Adam, our first father, sought to slake his thirst by other means—as with saltwater, which can never satisfy, even if it initially seems to please. Since that first fall, God made the Israelites a thirsty people. "As the deer longs for streams of water," they prayed in the psalms, "so my soul longs for you, O God. My soul thirsts for God, the living God" (Ps. 42:2–3). At the height of salvation history's prayer—literally and spiritually—the Second Adam echoes the first. From the Cross, God (that is, Jesus Christ) reaffirms His unquenched desire for us: "I thirst" (John 19:28). But this candid and even desperate expression of desire is also man's response to God. As man, Christ also enunciates His unslaked desire for our Father in heaven—God Almighty. God says to man, "I thirst" for you. Man says to God, "I thirst" for You. The words are simple, profound, and reflect the unity of the human and divine in Jesus Christ. The result? Water gushes forth from the tree of life,

---

[8] Cf. St. Augustine, *De diversis quaestionibus octoginta tribus* 64, 4:PL 40, 56.

quenching both divine and human thirst. In a similar way, as we make our journey through the Mass, we remember St. Augustine's words about prayer in general, and we suddenly see prayer as the pilgrim's watery oasis on the often dry and dusty way to heaven.

But as we examine this prayer in particular, the Opening Prayer of the Mass, we must understand that it is a particular type of plea and a specific kind of oasis. To stay on track during our journey, then, it is important that we keep in mind the unique properties of this verbal gateway to the Mass and how it differs from private prayer. In my private prayers, for example, I speak with God as my heart desires. I can address my prayer to the Father, or to the Son, or to the Holy Spirit, or to all three at once. I can speak to God from my heart about my current needs and loves—thanking Him for my morning meal of bacon and eggs or asking Him to grant me a winning Powerball ticket. I once read a charming story about a young girl who, after receiving her First Communion, returned to her pew and in her prayer thanked Jesus for her parents and siblings, recited twice to Him her ABCs, and ended by telling Him a ghost story. And why not? Private prayer ought to be as personalized as the one praying it. On the other hand, interestingly enough, when entering into private prayer, I can enjoy the presence of God and contemplate His goodness using no words at all. While you and I share a common thirst, God satisfies the dryness each of us experiences in our hearts according to our particular needs and wants.

Moving from private prayer to public worship—from our bedside each night to the church pews each Sunday—we must keep in mind a few other signposts on this journey into mystery. Most of the Mass's prayers, including the Opening Prayer, differ in some ways from private prayer, mostly because they are prayed by many people at once. Unless the family and friends at your birthday party, for example, sing "Happy Birthday" with the same words and the same melody (or close to it), the song will come out as a discordant disaster. Such unity is also vital for the success of public expressions of civic goodwill, such as the National Anthem, the Pledge of Allegiance, or your college team's fight song. Similarly, liturgical prayer, of which the Mass is the greatest example, requires the vocal unity of a group, an assembly, a body. But in the liturgical context, it is not just any body: any time Catholics join their voices together in Mass, it is nothing less than the Mystical Body of Christ, which speaks as one. You and I and Bill remain individuals at Mass, but we work and pray and travel together as a single Body. Recalling St. Augustine's figure for prayer as a driving force among pilgrims wandering the desert of this world, the Opening Prayer—if prayed with intention and intelligence—is an expresssion of individual and corporate thirst. But how, combining in a single prayer, can the Mystical Body of Christ quench our collective thirst?

The answer to this question is as simple and profound as the prayer itself. Following the Penitential Act and, on solemnities and most Sundays, the Gloria, the priest says, "Let us pray." When we looked at the church's doors and the Sign of the Cross, we took some time to uncover their meaning—both are sacramental things and can therefore be examined mystagogically. The invitation, "Let us pray," needs no disciplined treatment. The words mean what they say—simple, direct, and to the point: "Let us pray." Nevertheless, even this simple invitation, in my experience, often goes in one ear and out the other. What I—and every other individual in the assembly ought to do—is *pray*. We should not be waiting for the next "cue" from the missal, but even before the priest begins the formal prayer of the Mass we should be calling to mind our hearts' intentions. What do I want to ask of Jesus? What sorrows and struggles do I want to lay before Him? What favors and graces can I thank Him for? How can I express my love and adoration for Him? How much more truly unified in our "thirst" would the Mystical Body of Christ be if every soul in the assembly prayed in this way?

So it is that the pilgrims on the journey into the mystery of the Mass take their first major steps. Then, when all of the individual travelers in this mass exodus have called to mind their prayers, the priest, who is the head and leader of the body, collects them and, in one voice, offers them to the Father, through the Son, in the Holy Spirit. "Collect"—with the emphasis on the first syllable, "COL-lect"—is the traditional name for this Opening Prayer. Ideally, the individual desires of each cell of the Mystical Body are collected by their head and presented to the Father in one single "I thirst" expressed by the Mystical Body of Jesus. This is when exciting things start to happen on our journey: when the scenery fascinates, the detours and the road construction end, and we start cruising in the fast lane—ice-cold water at hand—to paradise.

But like the Chosen People, who too often didn't listen, or even as Moses, who led them imperfectly (and, because of his deafness to God's words, never did make it into the Promised Land), our own Opening Prayer may often lack the quenching quality it is meant to have. For two related reasons, the Opening Prayer is offered without this quality of liquid refreshment. First, the members of the assembly don't always offer the priest intentions for him to collect and offer as a way to satisfy God's thirst for us. Instead of a tidal wave of adoration, contrition, thanksgiving, and petition, Father is underwhelmed by a trickle—like the drinking fountain that dribbles a weak stream from its spigot. But even as the assembly would do well to admit their weak response to the priest's invitation, Father also bears some fault too. How many times have you been in Mass and heard the invitation to pray—only to be cut off mid-intention as the priest moves the Collect along at too quick a pace? Dialogue is important between priest and congregation, but so is allowing the assembly the silent pause necessary to call to mind its intentions.

Silence is an essential ingredient for both individual and corporate prayer, and recent popes have shouted about the importance of silence with increasing volume. Pope St. John Paul II, for example, taught that "we need silence 'if we are to accept in our hearts the full resonance of the voice of the Holy Spirit and to unite our personal prayer more closely to the Word of God and the public voice of the Church.'[9] In a society that lives at an increasingly frenetic pace, often deafened by noise and confused by the ephemeral, it is vital to rediscover the value of silence.... The Liturgy, with its different moments and symbols, cannot ignore silence."[10] His successor, Pope Benedict XVI, in an address to Carthusian monks, who live the majority of their days in silence, remarked that all of the noise of modern life has given "rise to talk about anthropological mutation. Some people are no longer able to remain for long periods in silence and solitude."[11] Appreciate what Benedict is saying here: too much noise and not enough silence makes me a monster—a mutant! Taking his cue from his predecessors, Pope Francis has also spoken about the

---

[9] *General Instruction of the Liturgy of the Hours*, 202.

[10] John Paul II, apostolic letter *Spiritus et Sponsa*, on the fortieth anniversary of the Constitution on the Sacred Liturgy (December 4, 2003), no. 13.

[11] Benedict XVI, homily at the Church of the Charterhouse of Serra San Bruno, October 9, 2011.

silent prayer of adoration. "We cannot know the Lord without this habit of worship, to worship in silence, adoration," he says. "Allow me to say this: waste time in front of the Lord, in front of the mystery of Jesus Christ. Worship him. There in silence, the silence of adoration."[12]

But the power of silence isn't an invention of the twenty-first-century Church. Like doors and crosses, silence can be understood in its fullness by looking to some of our mystagogical categories of meaning. For instance, even as moments of intentional silence fade in our modern day, "observing a moment of silence" after national tragedies and before large sporting events remains a powerful symbol of unity and recollection. (Can you imagine the outrage if one were to disrupt a silent moment at a 9-11 memorial ceremony with shouts or laughter?)

One place where silence is not silent is Scripture. As we should come to expect, God's word gives numerous examples of divine silence. The prophet Elijah—himself on a journey in the desert, and fed and watered by God's angel—finds himself conversing with God at the mouth of a cave atop Mount Horeb. How did the Lord sound? "There was a strong and violent wind rending the mountains and crushing rocks before the LORD—but the LORD was not in the wind; after the wind, an earthquake—but the LORD was not in the earthquake; after the earthquake, fire—but the LORD was not in the fire; after the fire, a light silent sound" (1 Kings 19:11–12). Only in silence did the Lord speak, and only in silence did Elijah hear him.

Later, atop Mount Tabor, Elijah and Moses appear with Jesus—they were speaking "of his exodus that he was going to

---

[12] Deborah Castellano Lubov, "Pope Tells 3 Ways to Know Christ at Morning Mass," Zenit, October 20, 2016.

accomplish in Jerusalem"—and Peter, James, and John see Jesus transfigured in glory. A voice speaks from the cloud that came to overshadow the apostles, telling them that this Jesus "is my chosen Son," and that they must "listen to him." Then, "after the voice had spoken, Jesus was found alone. They fell silent" (Luke 9:29–36). The presence of the glorified Lord calls for silence and in that silence a reflection (literally "bending back") of the God-man's brilliance in the world around us.

In heaven, the New Jerusalem even has its own moments of silence. Right before the seven trumpets blow, and before the wedding banquet gets into full swing, we hear that "there was silence in heaven for about half an hour" (Rev. 8:1). The Mass is a moment when heaven breaks into earth—or earth into heaven—and we reflect again the heavenly liturgy.

Truly, there is "a time to be silent, and a time to speak" (Eccles. 3:7), and the Opening Prayer is both. In silence, our prayers well up from our hearts and come to the forefront of our minds. Then, in the words of the Church, the priest gathers these prayers and offers them to the Father, through the Son, in the Holy Spirit. If God thirsts for us so that we might thirst for Him, the Opening Prayer satisfies God's thirst by quenching ours.

Our journey into the heart of the Mass, and, through it, to heaven, takes twists and turns, but it need not resemble forty years of desert suffering. Each of us who professes to be part of the Mystical Body of Christ must contribute to the journey. But like any trip on which many share the driving, so to speak, each of us is not expected to contribute everything on his own. Since you and I are joined with one another as pilgrims along the way, we speak and hear both in the shared silence of our hearts and in the voice of our leader and head. When the Opening Prayer is offered by one and many, in silence and in words, it signifies—it is a sign—that our journey is moving in the right direction.

The oasis that is the Opening Prayer accelerates our heart's path to God. In the Liturgy of the Word, which follows, our hearts hear God's voice calling us ever deeper to Himself. To help us hear more clearly the Father's good Word, in the next chapter we'll listen to the insights of two holy men who know firsthand what speaking and hearing well is all about.

In Brief

✦ Prayer is a conversation with God, a meeting centered on Jesus the Word, a mutual thirst and common satisfaction.

✦ Although personal prayer can use familiar words, such as the Our Father or the Hail Mary, it should also find expression in the silent or spoken words unique to every individual.

✦ The liturgical prayer of the Mystical Body of Christ is corporate and communal, often employing words and images appropriate to the many individuals who compose the Body.

✦ The Opening Prayer, or Collect, requires both the individual contributions—the pleas of each member of the Body—and a leader or head to gather them and give them to God the Father in a single voice.

✦ Silence, both within the liturgy and outside of it, is necessary to hear God's voice and to formulate our intentions and desires for God.

THE NEXT TIME YOU GO TO MASS

✦ Before Mass, formulate your intentions—sentiments of adoration, sorrow, thanksgiving, and petition. When the priest says, "Let us pray," consciously bring these intentions forward so that he can offer them—and everybody else's—to God.

✦ Be silent on the way to Mass and before Mass and, like Elijah atop Mount Horeb or the Apostles before the Transfigured Christ, strive to listen in silence to God's voice.

✦ Read the Mass's Opening Prayer beforehand. It will indicate the character of the day's celebration and may inspire your thirst for a prayerful encounter with God.

✦ Pray the Opening Prayer from the Sunday Mass throughout the week. The Living Water we find at Mass isn't contained in a twelve-ounce bottle. Rather, the Mass is the fount of our spiritual life, and drinking from this infinite source of grace will continue to nourish us throughout the week.

4

How to Listen to the Readings

✠

The LORD would speak to Moses face to face,
as a person speaks to a friend.

—Exodus 33:11

Fifth-century Rome was not the beautiful place it is today. This powerful city, the political and cultural capital of an empire that for centuries had maintained peace through military might, had slowly but steadily declined into a den of violence and vice. Political leadership was decided often by assassination or bribery—or both. Out-of-work farmers, who were once the backbone of the empire, flooded the city in need of housing, food, and medicine. Prostitution and the deadly games of the Coliseum were principal forms of entertainment. Lead pipes furnishing water to the city's wealthy caused blood poisoning. The army, now largely manned by foreign troops, was expensive and not entirely devoted to preserving the city and the empire. Finally, in 476, the last emperor of the Western Roman Empire, Romulus Augustus, was overthrown by the barbarian King Odoacer—and the decline and fall of the Roman Empire was now history.

At this same time, in the outskirts of Rome, in a town called Nursia, the future St. Benedict was born. The son of a noble family, Benedict spent his boyhood studying in Rome until, around the year 500, too often tempted by the city's vices and his friends' lifestyles, he left the city for a place more conducive to the life of faith and virtue. Gathering around himself other like-minded men, the "Father of Western Monasticism" would compose a "rule of life" that would bring order and beauty out of the chaos and ugliness of the time. For those who followed his Rule, life was redirected to God; for those of us today who want to hear God's voice in the midst of our own chaos, St. Benedict is a perfect patron.

Benedict, whose name means "to speak well" (from the Latin *bene* and *dicere*), embodies that ultimate benediction and good Word of the Father, Jesus. The first line of St. Benedict's famous *Rule* echoes the blessed meaning of his name. He begins simply, yet profoundly: "Listen, my child, with the ear of your heart." It's an odd image, if taken literally—picture your heart growing a pair of rabbit ears—but as a metaphor for prayerfulness, the image speaks to the core of what we are after as we listen to the readings during the Liturgy of the Word. Considering how often we hear without listening, we might ask what we can do to keep the Word of God from going in one ear and out the other. (Have you ever responded "Thanks be to God" at the end of a reading, only to realize that you could not name one thing mentioned in the reading?) How can I take the "good speech" of God into my heart so that, upon entering my bloodstream, so to speak, it extends through my body's arteries and veins to all extremities and animates my whole being? In other words, how can I hear the Word of God as St. Benedict did, so that, like him, I might be a saint in the midst of our challenging times?

With the Second Vatican Council, the Church has refocused on how she should proclaim the Word of God to her members. In numerous places in the Council's documents, and now in the ritual books mandated by their reform, the Magisterium speaks of the "table of the word" and the "nourishment" it brings to hearts with ears.[13] Recall the image of the angel in the book of Revelation who gave St. John a scroll to eat, and it gives new meaning to a substantial word that you can sink your teeth into! To help us understand the Church's theology of the word, here are two of the many truths we should keep in mind so that we may hear the Liturgy of the Word as the Church desires.

First, like all things sacramental (such as the elements we previously discussed—doors, crosses, and silence), we should know that the substance of the liturgical word—each scriptural sentence and every liturgical syllable—is, chapter and verse, Jesus, the Word. The beginning of St. John's Gospel captures this truth clearly. Called the Prologue, which means "before the word," the Evangelist proclaims, "In the beginning was the Word, and the Word was with God, and the Word was God" (John 1:1). When we reflected on the Sign of the Cross, we heard that it was through this Word that the Father and the Spirit created all things: "God said ..." (see Gen. 1). Proclaiming this same word to the Lord's Chosen People, the Old Testament prophets sought to redirect the Israelites' hearts to God. For, as even the Jews understood, by the wise word of the Father, God "appeared on earth" and was "at home with mortals" (Bar. 3:38). To this degree, Jews and Catholics understand how important the "word" is to prayer and liturgy. But all these words of the Old Testament reveal a single word, the first and last word of the New Testament.

---

[13] See, for example, the *Introduction to the Lectionary for Mass.*

When deaf and fallen hearts had been suitably formed to hear God's voice again in the fullness of time, the Word even "became flesh" to live visibly and audibly among us (see John 1:14). With his stunning poetic sensibilities, St. Ephrem of Syria (d. 373), a deacon and Doctor of the Church, even suggested a "double incarnation" of Jesus: not only did the Son of God become a Son of Mary, uniting His divine nature with our human nature, but this same "Word of God" also united Himself with the "words of man." Thus, to hear and say and pray the Scriptural Word is to hear and say and pray the Eternal Word. The liturgical word is brimming over with the Divine Word—and this truth should prick our heart's ears.

A second point to help us hear the Liturgy of the Word more fruitfully follows upon the truth that liturgical words sound like the Divine Word. We know that in the beginning God created all things through His Word, but that through sin, our first parents closed their ears and hearts to it, choosing instead to listen to lies. Not abandoning His beloved creation to its own devices, God continued to speak to His people, even if at times "in partial and various ways" through His prophets. Consequently, since fallen and finite ears don't hear as well as those infused with the perfect pitch of God's grace, the Chosen People also offered only an imperfect response—and would reply to God not directly but through their priests. But with the Incarnation of Jesus, "He spoke to us through a son" (Heb. 1:1–2). Then, in the person of Jesus, salvation history's conversation between heaven and earth, the face-to-face, mouth-to-mouth encounter between God and man, is restored. That is, in the incarnate Christ, God (who Jesus is) speaks clearly, lovingly, and convincingly, while man (which Jesus is) hears perfectly and responds wholeheartedly. The first dialogue that united Creator and creation, interrupted by the deafness of the first Adam, has been restored by Jesus, the Second Adam—and a new creation has been born.

As we consider this restored discourse of Creator and creation, here is the remarkable part: history's conversation between God and humanity is not something lost to the past, nor is it that magnificent story happening beyond my day-to-day (or Mass-to-Mass) experience. Quite the contrary: the Mass's Liturgy of the Word is a microcosm of the great story of salvation history. Consider the first act of the Liturgy of the Word, the reading from the Old Testament. Like the Chosen People, God speaks to us, yet distantly and, at times, in the shadowy figures of the luminous Christ yet to come. Then, in the psalm response, we speak to God, not in our own language, but in that of the Scriptures. The second reading finds God speaking to us again, now more clearly and closely, in light of Jesus. In the Gospel, Jesus speaks to us Himself, while in the homily, with the aid of the Holy Spirit, His Body, the Church, opens up the mystery to willing hearts. What follows next is the Creed, in which it is our turn once again to respond to God, to assent to all He has revealed to us in His Word heard in the preceding readings. Finally, in the Universal Prayer (also known as the General Intercessions) we speak to God, now in our own words, and intercede on behalf of the world. We should hear, then, in the Liturgy of the Word at Mass, an echo of salvation history's larger dialogue, and also an invitation for each of us to take part personally. Unlike those "stiff-necked" and hard-of-hearing hearts of the Old Covenant (which we may be tempted to look upon with disdain), we must listen to God with the ears of our hearts.

Before discussing practical ways in which we can develop this wholehearted hearing, let's look at one more point that speaks of the heart's role in the Liturgy of the Word. Just as history led to the high point of the incarnate Jesus speaking and hearing words of love from the Cross, so too the Liturgy of the Word reaches its climax as the liturgy moves from the Gospel to the Creed, before concluding with Universal Prayer. The Mass's Lectionary, the book that contains the readings for the Liturgy of the Word, describes the "dialogue between God and his people taking place through the Holy Spirit ... as an opportunity to take the word of God to heart and to prepare a response to it in prayer."[14] Only when we have taken the word of God to heart—hearing with the ear of the heart—can we respond with a heartfelt response, as Jesus did. Our first response to Jesus the Word after the Gospel is the Creed. The English word "creed" comes from the Latin *credo*, meaning "I believe." Some suggest *credo* is made up of two smaller words: *cor* is the word for "heart," as in "coronary" or "cordially," and *do* means "I give" and is the origin of "donate." Thus, the words "I believe" are no simple nod to what God says in the readings—as we might give to listening to the country station versus talk radio. Rather, saying "I believe" is putting one's whole heart on the line for the Word of God just heard. If I have heard with the ear of the heart, I can then give myself wholeheartedly back to God: "I believe"—which is the response He wishes to hear.

But the heart's work in the Mass isn't finished after hearing the Divine Word and responding to it. Its final task in this segment of the Mass is to intercede for the needs of the world, the Church, the community, and our families in the Universal Prayer. Offering prayers to God for others is a priestly action, and a priest is the mediator, the go-between, of two parties. We offer

---

[14] *Introduction to the Lectionary* 28.

the needs of others to God from our own hearts and, conversely, become channels of God's grace to the world. As our physical heart is the means by which lifeblood extends to the body and then returns for vital oxygen, so too our hearts are the conduits through which the world gasps for God's love and from which that love reaches others. Within the structure of the Mass, the Liturgy of the Word parallels the Liturgy of the Eucharist. Just as the Liturgy of the Eucharist reaches its high point in the worthy reception of Holy Communion, the Liturgy of the Word reaches its zenith in the Universal Prayer. Both actions represent the heart's desire for God, while both Communion and intercession fill the heart with divine life.

Fifteen hundred years ago, St. Benedict called us to listen with the ears of our hearts. More recently, another Benedict, Pope Benedict XVI, has reminded us how to carry on this work that the saint from Nursia made central in furthering the mission of the Western Church. The Church continues to teach us how to open the ears of our own hearts. Pope Benedict calls the Church "the great teacher of the art of listening,"[15] because she instructs her students, the Catholic faithful, on the often-difficult work of opening our ears and hearts. In particular, Pope Benedict writes about *lectio divina* (divine reading), one of the Church's preferred methods of praying Sacred Scripture. According to Pope Benedict, this method requires "the diligent reading of Sacred Scripture accompanied by prayer [which] brings about that intimate dialogue in which the person reading hears God who is speaking, and in praying, responds to him with trusting

---

[15] Benedict XVI, post-synodal apostolic exhortation *Verbum Domini* (September 30, 2010), no. 51.

openness of heart."[16] Benedict continues, "If it is effectively pro-
moted, this practice will bring to the Church—I am convinced
of it—a new spiritual springtime."[17]

Here is how *lectio divina* works.

Reading

The first step in the method of divine reading consists in se-
lecting and reading a particular text. Although any passage of
Scripture can be an encounter with God and a means to converse with Him, those from the Mass, especially the Gospel of
the coming Sunday's Mass, should be among our first choices.
We will discover, especially as we become accustomed to the
method of divine reading, that texts in which God's Word is
most explicit—that is, in the incarnate Christ—and where we
can more easily see and hear Him in our mind's eye and ear are
the most helpful.

With our scriptural selection in hand, we can begin reading.
Unlike most of our reading, which is done quickly, this inspired
Word—remember, it is ultimately Jesus in these words—is read
slowly and carefully. What does the text say in itself? What does
the Church—the teacher of the art of listening—want us to
hear? As a good teacher, the Church knows that repetition is the
mother of all learning. So, after reading the text the first time,
read it again—and again.

---

[16] Ibid.

[17] Benedict XVI, Address to the participants in the international congress
organized to commemorate the fortieth anniversary of the Dogmatic
Constitution on Divine Revelation *Dei Verbum* September 16, 2005.

The proclamation of the Gospel at Mass gives us a few insights for fruitful reading. Before the Gospel proclamation, the priest prepares himself by prayer, saying: "Cleanse my heart and my lips, almighty God, that I may worthily proclaim your holy Gospel." Similarly, we should begin our sacred reading with prayer. Although any genuine prayer will suffice, we might consider one based on the priest's own: "Cleanse my heart and my *ears*, almighty God, that I may worthily *read* Your holy Gospel." Next, during the Mass's Gospel reading, the priest or deacon stands, a posture that both expresses and fosters attention and respect. We don't have to stand during our sacred reading, but we ought to find a posture conducive to attentiveness and reflection—a posture, that is, free from distraction and disturbance. Finally, at the conclusion of the Gospel reading at Mass, the priest or deacon kisses the Book of the Gospels as a sign of love. To signify our heart's love for Christ the Word, we might consider a similar gesture in our own treatment of the sacred page.

Reflection

The second step in our divine reading is reflection. If we have read the passage slowly and repeatedly, in a place free from distraction and accompanied by prayer, the movement from reading to reflection will come naturally (or, if you like, supernaturally). If our concern during the first phase of divine reading inspired us to ask, "What does the passage say in itself?", then in reflection we might ask "What does the text say *to me*?" Unlike a blog, an e-mail, a magazine, or a book meant simply to convey basic information, Sacred Scripture facilitates a heart-to-heart communion with God. Its words are filled with the Word. Jesus is speaking loud and clear to the ears of our hearts.

The imagination is the best hearing aid at this time. Picture yourself in the scriptural passage before you. Are you one of the apostles who accompany Jesus and observes His works? Perhaps you are a nameless bystander who witnesses the healing of the paralytic. Have you come to hear Jesus with the crowds only to find yourself being fed by the miraculously multiplied loaves and fishes? Maybe you are a particular figure before Him, such as the diminutive Zacchaeus at the base of the sycamore tree or the high priest Caiaphas overseeing the trial of Jesus. Or imagine you are Jesus Himself carrying the Cross—what would He have experienced? By placing ourselves in the Gospel passage with as much detail as possible, we can reflect more clearly—and hear more deeply—the Word of the Father, who comes to us.

Response

After we read and reflect on the Gospel passage, the third move-ment in divine reading calls us to respond. As we saw above, neither salvation history nor the Liturgy of the Word that re-flects it are monologues, where only (*mono*) God does the talking (*logue*). God does indeed want us to listen, but He also wants our response: He desires a dialogue, a speaking back and forth across the divide that still separates us. If we have heard the Lord speaking to us in the scriptural text, what can we say to Him in return? If the Word tells us that we must be more generous (like the widow who gave her last penny), less ambitious (like James and John, who sought places next to Christ in glory), quick to forgive (as Jesus did from the Cross), or confidently trusting (like the blind men seeking sight from Jesus)—or any of a thousand things Jesus wishes to speak to us—how will we respond? Words responding in praise, thanksgiving, petition, or adoration, or even silent prayer are suitable. God reveals Himself, says Pope Benedict, as a "dialogue of love between the divine persons."[18] Our conversation with Christ at this point is His invitation and our acceptance to join in the divine dialogue.

Contemplation

A fourth step contemplates the dialogue that has taken place between my heart and Jesus' heart. Can you recall the great conversations in your life? I think back and hear clearly my future wife's response the morning I asked her to marry me. On another occasion, I can hear our doctor offering a hard diagnosis regarding a difficult pregnancy. I also recall the bittersweet parting words of a bishop I served before he was reassigned to another diocese. Each memory recalls a remarkable conversation; yet none of these discussions in my life is quite so extraordinary as a prayerful dialogue with Christ. Contemplating this heart-to-heart talk—be it comforting, challenging, or encouraging—helps me see the world and my place in it in a new light, just as I gained a new perspective from becoming a joyful fiancé, a worried father, or a grateful friend. St. Paul's Letter to the Romans calls us not to be conformed to this world—be it fifth-century Rome or twenty-first-century New York—but to "be transformed by the renewal of our mind" (12:2) so that we may see by the light of Christ—the same light that illuminates saints in the eternal city of the heavenly Jerusalem.

---

[18] Benedict XVI, *Verbum Domini* 6.

Resolution

A fifth and final step of divine reading is the resolve to act. The dialogue with the divine not only renews the mind, as St. Paul says, but renews all aspects of life, making us "living sacrifices," a key Catholic concept we'll unfold in the next chapter. St. Irenaeus of Lyon (d. 202) remarked that the "glory of God is man fully alive," and that this abundant life is born from "the vision of God." To see God face-to-face — or, for our purposes, to hear and converse with Him heart to heart — gives life. Our interactions with our siblings, children, co-workers, spouses, and each man on the street are now infused with grace and elevated to a higher plane. Conversing with Jesus moves our hearts, and our hearts move our bodies, and our bodies become living cells that move the Mystical Body ever closer to its full stature. The circumstances of each life will determine how we affect others, and it is necessary for each of us to ask at the end of our divine reading: "What concrete conversion of life is the Word calling me to?" Like the blessed Benedict who heard the Word with the ear of his heart, our own hearing transforms and divinizes us and, through us, those we encounter in the details of daily life. We may not be called to plant monasteries throughout the Italian countryside, but by praying with the Word of God, we ought to be inspired to do *something* magnificent for the sake of God.

In review, the process of divine reading (*lectio divina*) includes:

+ *Reading:* How do I engage the text at hand — preferably the coming Sunday's Gospel — through a slow, prayerful, reading and rereading of the text?

+ *Reflection:* What is Jesus, the Word, saying to me through the text?

✦ *Response:* How do I reply in sentiments of love, adoration, thanksgiving, or supplication to Jesus?

✦ *Contemplation:* What things do I consider after the divine conversation that has just taken place and the spiritual insights it gives?

✦ *Resolution:* What actions has this reading inspired me to carry out in the life opening before me in the week ahead?

Although the method does require effort, the work it involves always yields spiritual fruit. The Mass's proclamation of the Word is indeed powerful, but to benefit from such power, we the faithful ought to pray with the passage in the days leading up to Mass and in the days following. When our ears and hearts have been attuned to the Sunday Gospel passage, its words have more emotional punch, greater spiritual force, and keener meaning for us.

Finally, divine reading is suitable not only for individuals but for families. Of course, when dealing with an entity as fluid as a family, it's always good to have a plan. Whether alone or with others, consider reading and rereading next Sunday's Gospel on the Tuesday before the Lord's Day. On the next day, Wednesday, read the passage again and begin the second step of reflection: What is God saying to me as a father and husband? Then I might ask my son Dominic, "What is He saying to you?" Or I might ask my daughter Helen, "What are you hearing in the Word?" On Thursday, put step 3 into words: "What do I say to God in return?" I'll ask my son Laurence, "What do you say to Jesus?" On Friday, the family may read and rest in the conversation unfolding before it, and on Saturday, individually or together, either privately or publicly, family members commit to changing specific elements in their lives for the better. When Sunday comes around, it will be impossible to hear the Gospel reading with deafness, inattention, or passivity. A true encounter with God will take place.

St. Benedict encourages us to hear with the ear of our heart, and divine reading helps us to do it. Our next chapter will help us prepare the "heart of our heart" for sacrifice, and the humble yet spirited trio of Hananiah, Azariah, and Mishael will show us how from the depths of a fiery furnace.

In Brief

+ The Word of God is not simply texts and words spoken at Mass, but first and foremost is a Person, the Word of the Trinity. All liturgical words, in some way, make audible this divine Word.

+ The Mass's Liturgy of the Word resembles history's larger economy of salvation: just as the Father conversed with the Chosen People through the prophets, so now does the conversation continue back and forth between God and His people in the readings.

+ The high point of the Liturgy of the Word is the heartfelt response to the Father in the Creed, followed by our offering the world and its needs to God in the Universal Prayer.

+ The method of divine reading—consisting of reading, reflecting, responding, contemplating, and acting—is the Church's sure way to take the Word of God to heart and respond in love from the heart.

✦ The Gospel for Sunday Mass can best be heard and lived by praying over it, either individually or collectively, during the week preceding its proclamation during Sunday Mass.

THE NEXT TIME YOU GO TO MASS

✦ Find next Sunday's reading, either in the parish missalette, a monthly resource (e.g., *Magnificat*), or online (e.g., http://www.usccb.org/bible/readings).

✦ In the days leading up to Sunday, follow the process of *lectio divina*: reading, reflecting, responding, contemplating, acting.

✦ In the day or two following the Sunday hearing of the Word, recall the Gospel message and thank God for the fruits received from its prayerful hearing in your heart.

5

How to Prepare the Heart at the Offertory

✠

Were not our hearts burning within us?

—Luke 24:32

Even God enjoys a tongue twister every once in a while. Take, for example, the three young men we encounter in the book of Daniel. The names Shadrach, Meshach, and Abednego may strike fear into the heart of the parish lector, but they ought to warm the heart of the parish priest. These three young men—often called by their Hebrew names of Hananiah, Mishael, and Azariah, just to keep you guessing—were thrown into a fiery furnace for refusing to worship a ninety-foot-tall golden statue erected by the Babylonian king Nebuchadnezzar. The story, recounted in chapter 3 of the book of Daniel, isn't read once during the three-year cycle of Sunday readings. Yet its message, as well as its central text (verses 39–40), is present at every Mass during the preparation of the altar and the gifts. This is truly right and just because the three youths exemplify the only true way for the Church to prepare for the Eucharistic sacrifice.

Given the secular and selfish state of today's culture, "sacrifice" is not an especially popular activity. But even among those who understand its importance—today and at all times—there is some disagreement about what "sacrifice" means. Pope Benedict said that the concept of sacrifice "has been buried under the debris of endless misunderstandings."[19] We might ask ourselves: "How do I understand the meaning of sacrifice?" It's a question we cannot afford to get wrong, especially since the heart of Jesus' ministry was His *sacrifice* on the Cross. That same heart beats at the center of the Mass in the *sacrifice* made present in the Eucharist. Moreover, our baptismal calling requires us to offer ourselves as a *sacrifice*. To misunderstand the true sense of sacrifice is to miss the very meaning of life as a Catholic.

At first glance, Sacred Scripture doesn't appear to offer any clarity about sacrifice. In numerous places, God the Father seems to suggest that He's not interested in sacrifice. For example, after Saul, the king of Israel, defeats Amalek in battle, he returns home with choice lambs and oxen to sacrifice to the Lord—despite the fact that the Lord commanded Saul to destroy all that Amalek possessed, including "oxen and sheep, camels and donkeys." God did not want such sullied sacrifice. Rather, God's prophet Samuel tells Saul, "Obedience is better than sacrifice" (1 Sam. 15:22). Likewise, living in the last days of the Northern Kingdom before its destruction by the Assyrians around 720 B.C., the prophet Hosea compares the tribes of Israel to his estranged spouse. He hears the Lord calling His people to fidelity: "For it is loyalty that I desire, not sacrifice, and knowledge of God rather than burnt offerings" (Hos. 6:6). A similar rebuke of "sacrifice" comes through

---

[19] Joseph Cardinal Ratzinger (Benedict XVI), *The Spirit of the Liturgy* (San Francisco: Ignatius Press, 2014), 27.

the psalmist. "Do I eat the flesh of bulls or drink the blood of he-goats? Offer praise as your sacrifice to God" (Ps. 50:13–14). From these passages, it seems that God wishes obedience, loyalty, and praise—but none of that messy business of sacrifice.

But do these passages then indicate that Jesus died without cause? Why would He offer Himself in sacrifice if God the Father doesn't wish it? Jesus speaks in a similar way when rebuked by the Pharisees for choosing Matthew as an apostle and dinner companion: "Those who are well do not need a physician," he retorts, "but the sick do. Go and learn the meaning of the words, 'I desire mercy, not sacrifice.' I did not come to call the righteous but sinners." (Matt. 9:12–13). Besides being messy, sacrifice can also be a confusing business.

The common view of sacrifice, the one "buried under the debris of endless misunderstandings," is closely related to the kind of sacrifice the Lord seems to reject in the Old Testament. To illustrate, consider that familiar question most Catholics are asking in the days leading up to Ash Wednesday: "What will I give up for Lent this year?" Even though this question is often the focus of a pastor's sermon to his parishioners, pre-Lenten dinnertime discussion among parents and children, and a query that we each ask in a personal way as part of our preparation for the forty-day season, this perennial question perpetuates an incomplete view of sacrifice. Indeed, most of us, most of the time, associate "sacrifice" with giving up, going without, destruction, deprivation, loss, pain, and suffering. If we focus so absolutely on these unpleasant aspects of sacrifice, we are consequently tempted to "sacrifice" to God things that are small, those that are not essential to us, gifts that are on the heart's periphery and disconnected from the core of our being—and all in a way that duty demands. Sound familiar?

But anyone who ever has sacrificed, in even a small way, can rightly object: sacrifices *are* painful and they *do* involve going without. The Mass's Fourth Eucharistic Prayer even says that, to accomplish the Father's plan, Jesus "gave himself up to death." And who would care to tell Jesus that His sacrifice on the Cross was not agonizing or destructive? In fact, the Church and her Tradition agree that sacrifice can be painful, deprivative, and destructive. But if we think these elements are at the essence of sacrifice, then we aren't seeing the whole picture — or even the most important parts of the picture.

Imagine Jesus' sacrifice on the Cross — but try to visualize it through the eyes of God the Father. What is it about His Son's action that satisfies Him? Why is it that salvation is now possible through the Son's sacrifice? How does Calvary's Crucifixion reconcile us to the Father? It is not, God the Father would probably answer, because humanity has inflicted pain and suffering on His Son, torturing and killing Him, "sacrificing" (in the incomplete sense of the term) Him in our place. Even while these aspects of Christ's offering are present, there is something deeper.

That something deeper is the heart of sacrifice: the heart of man. God wants nothing else. Beneath the pain, loss, deprivation, and destruction associated with Jesus' offering, our Lord's Sacred Heart desires nothing more than loving union with God the Father. In Psalm 50, God says: "For every animal of the forest is mine, beasts by the thousands on my mountains. I know every bird in the heights; whatever moves in the wild is mine. Were I hungry, I would not tell you, for mine is the world and all that fills it" (10–13). In other words, as Job could have told the psalmist, God has the power to take to Himself everything from man: body, mind, health, family, memory, job, sight, clothes, material luxuries. But there is one thing that this all-powerful God is powerless to take. This one thing He can only have if it is freely given to Him: the undivided love of man. And (wouldn't you know it!) this is the one thing He really wants. (And to think my sacrificing vanilla ice cream [not chocolate] for Lent [except on Sundays] would satisfy Him!)

For this reason, Pope Benedict's reflections on the true nature of sacrifice are vital to preparing our hearts for Mass. Benedict doesn't simply point out our deficient misunderstandings, that at its core "sacrifice has nothing to do with destruction" (34), but he shows what sacrifice truly is: "love-transformed mankind" (28), "in its essence simply returning to love and therefore divinization" (33), "growth in love" (33), "transformation into love" (47), and "humanity becoming love with Christ" (76). God the Father wants a loving union with you and me, whole and entire, with nothing kept back by us. If I offer words of prayer, these are acceptable because my heart is in some real way present in them. If I put a twenty-dollar bill in the collection basket, it is welcomed by God—but only if it comes from my heart. If I give up chocolate ice cream for Lent, this small sacrifice is received only when attached to my heart's undivided desire for union with the Trinity. It was this same devotion to the Father and His will—a devotion amplified by His willingness to endure pain and suffering—that made Christ's sacrifice pleasing to the Father.

Besides serving as a guidepost for each of us on our spiritual journey, this fundamental truth about sacrifice also plays an important role in communal liturgy. The preparation of the gifts at Mass is really a preparation for sacrifice. Therefore, our understanding of true sacrifice should lead each participant at Mass to prepare for the sacrifice by asking a single question: "How can I get my whole self onto the altar—even onto the paten holding the host and into the chalice of wine—to give to God?" At the conclusion of the preparation of the altar and the gifts, the priest will command us to "pray that my sacrifice *and yours* may be acceptable to God, the almighty Father." This juncture along our journey into the Mass is the moment when we are asked to make our sacrifice. It is the time to carry our sacrificial gifts—ourselves—to the altar.

Let's look at sacrifice in another way. The prayer called the Morning Offering, especially if prayed daily, can assist any who wish to sacrifice themselves with Jesus to the Father in the Holy Spirit. One version of the Morning Offering begins, "O Jesus, through the Immaculate Heart of Mary, I offer you my prayers, works, joys, and sufferings of this day in union with the Holy Sacrifice of the Mass throughout the world." Think of someone you know intimately, either your spouse or a child or a best friend. The intimacy between you and this person comes in part from a shared knowledge of essential and innermost secrets and sensibilities, foibles and fears, desires and loves. Here's what most people know about me. I am 6 feet, 180 pounds (or thereabout), a resident of Wisconsin, and a father of eight. While these facts about me are true and important, they only begin to reveal who I am. Were I to reveal to you all that I work for either professionally or personally, all that I pray for large or small, all that brings me joy, all that I suffer, all that I fear, all that I hope, all the sinful things I do, all that I desire, then you would have knowledge of me in a way that mere facts cannot communicate. It is these essential details about me—or, put simply, "me"—that God wants.

During the preparation of the altar and the gifts at Mass, then, consider slowly and thoughtfully what or whom you pray for; what you are working toward in the days, weeks, months, and years to come; what has brought you recent joy; and each thing large or small that causes you pain or suffering. Be specific and genuine in these considerations, for these secrets of the heart represent you—the you that God wants.

With this sense of sacrifice in mind, let's go to Mass. We've reached that part in the liturgy known as the Presentation of the Gifts. As the monetary collection, the bread, and the wine are brought forward, imagine that your prayers, works, joys, and sufferings are carried forward too. The priest takes your spiritual offerings to the altar and joins them to everybody else's in the church building—and everybody's around the world. All of these intentions—which, recall, truly represent the heart's desire for God—are joined together with the sacrificial offering of Jesus.

You may have noticed, for example, that when the chalice is prepared, the priest or deacon adds a small amount of water to the wine. There are a number of practical and spiritual interpretations of this action—one of them sees the wine as Christ's sacrifice and the water as our sacrifice. In the chalice, we join ourselves (all our prayers, works, joys, and sufferings) to Jesus. The offering of the bread for the Eucharist can be understood in a similar way. An ancient text called the *Didache* (around A.D. 100) speaks of bread or grain scattered on the hillsides that comes together to make one lump of dough or a single loaf of bread. These various "grains" or fractions of bread on the paten can be understood as the individual members of the Mystical Body of Christ taking part in the ultimate sacrifice. The bread on the paten is, as it were, made up of my prayers, your works, Mrs. Murphy's joys, and Deacon Stephen's sufferings. These grains all join together and, along with Christ's sacrifice, are offered to the Father. What power there is in Christ's Mystical Body when each person in the church building presents such an offering to God!

We left our three young men in danger of death in Nebuchadnezzar's white-hot furnace. We return to them now, again to show how they serve as models for us as we prepare to sacrifice. Shadrach, Meshach, and Abednego were Jews living in Babylon following the conquest of Judah in the sixth century B.C. Taken from Jerusalem, the captive Israelites were deprived of their Temple, their priesthood, and animals for offering to God. All of the normative ways established by God to relate rightly to Him were destroyed. So when Shadrach, Meshach, and Abednego find themselves in the fiery furnace and realize their serious predicament, Abednego acknowledges and bemoans the fact that they "are reduced, O Lord, beyond any other nation, brought low everywhere in the world this day because of our sins. We have in our day no prince, prophet, or leader, no burnt offering, sacrifice, oblation, or incense, no place to offer first fruits, to find favor with you" (Dan. 3:37–38). Putting it plainly, the three young men have nothing to sacrifice to God and thus win deliverance.

Well, almost nothing.

Reaching into the heart of their very selves, Abednego continues: "But with contrite heart and humble spirit let us be received; as though it were burnt offerings of rams and bulls, or tens of thousands of fat lambs, so let our sacrifice be in your presence today and find favor before you; for those who trust in you cannot be put to shame. And now we follow you with our whole heart" (Dan. 3:39–41). The only thing the three have to offer is "humble spirits and contrite hearts"—which is precisely what God wanted in the first place.

While we may never literally face the flames of a furnace in our moments of prayer, our offering at Mass is the same as that of this trio from Daniel: God wants our humble spirits and contrite hearts. The priest will even pray Abednego's prayer after preparing the bread and wine—and you—on the altar. Although in a low voice, inaudible to all in the pews, he bows low and prays: "With humble spirit and contrite heart may we be accepted by you, O Lord, and may our sacrifice in your sight this day be pleasing to you, Lord God." In a spiritual sense, then, the church building becomes a fiery furnace, filled with hearts burning with love for God. These join with the Sacred Heart of Jesus and, in virtue of His heart, are given to the Father in heaven.

The Holy Spirit, prefigured in the breeze of the fiery furnace and invoked during Mass, will help us offer living sacrifices. Following the prayer in which Abednego offered the Lord his and his compatriots' humble and contrite hearts, the Lord "made the inside of the furnace as though a dew-laden breeze were blowing through it. The fire in no way touched them or caused them pain or harm" (Daniel 3:50). In the Old Testament, images of clouds (such as that which covered the Tent of Meeting during the desert exodus), wind (sweeping over the waters on day 1 of the world's creation), and water (which the prophet Ezekiel says creates a new heart and gives a new spirit) prefigure God the Holy Spirit. The "dew-laden breeze," also a type of the Holy Spirit, is the sign of the Father's acceptance of Shadrach's, Meshach's, and Abednego's loving hearts. This same dew-laden breeze arrives at each Mass, animating and transforming our sacrifices so that they may be acceptable to God the Father. This image of the Holy Spirit shows up in the Second Eucharistic Prayer as the priest asks the Father to "make holy, therefore, these gifts, we pray, by sending down your Spirit upon them like the dewfall." The combination of our prayers, works, joys, and sufferings joined with the sacrifice of Jesus present in the Mass, and transformed by the Holy Spirit, becomes the true sacrificial gift desired by God.

Shadrach, Meshach, Abednego: don't let their names frighten you. Rather, at the preparation of the gifts at Mass, imagine yourself sitting alongside them—as well as Steve, Betty, Laurence, and Mrs. Murphy—all gathered together in the fiery furnace of the church's nave.

More often than not, at collection time during Mass, the ushers are moving along the pews brandishing a basket with a long handle. But they could just as well be handing out a collection plate. It is not accidental that the Latin word for "plate" is *paten*, which is also the proper name for the gold dish that holds the host at Mass. So when the collection basket, or plate, comes through the nave, place yourself in (or on) it. Offer up all that is good and bad and ugly—all that you are—so that you can find yourself united with others in Jesus' own body, transformed by the Spirit, and offered in loving union to the Father. This offering will be a true gift to God, one that He is unable to have without you.

Preparing the gift of self is essential at Mass, but so is having the power to offer that self to God. Before Christ's coming, the people were powerless to offer sacrifices on their own; they had to give them to a special body of priests, the Levites, to give to God. Now, because of our unity with Jesus in baptism, all members of the Church are priests and share in the priestly work of the ordained priest. But that's not to say the ministerial priesthood is an afterthought. In our next chapter, we'll consider how an offering needs a priest, and what one has to do with the other. It may be the most exciting part of the journey into the Mass thus far.

In Brief

+ "Sacrifice," which is at the heart of Jesus' saving work, the Mass, and the Christian life, means giving undivided love to God the Father.

+ Sacrificial gifts and offerings that truly represent the heart of the giver are the true sacrifice God desires. If, rather than representing the heart, they merely replace or "stand in" for the heart, God is less interested, since He has these things already.

+ The objective of the preparation of the gifts and of the altar is to place our whole selves on the altar so that we can be joined with Jesus' whole self (Body, Blood, Soul, and Divinity) and given to God the Father.

+ A daily reflection, aided by the Morning Offering (see below), will prepare us to give ourselves with Jesus to the Father during Mass.

+ The Holy Spirit is present at Mass, just as He was in the fiery furnace and on the Cross of Calvary, and He assists in our preparation of self.

THE NEXT TIME YOU GO TO MASS

✦ Pray the Morning Offering thoughtfully and reflectively each morning during the week:

> O Jesus, through the Immaculate Heart of Mary, I offer you my prayers, works, joys, and sufferings of this day in union with the Holy Sacrifice of the Mass throughout the world. I offer them for all the intentions of your Sacred Heart: the salvation of souls, the reparation for sin, and the reunion of all Christians. I offer them for the intentions of our bishops and of all Apostles of Prayer, and in particular for those recommended by our Holy Father this month.

✦ Recall your prayers, works, joys, and sufferings on the way to Mass, either individually or as a family.

✦ Pray to the Holy Spirit — the dew of grace — to move your heart and prepare it for union with God, for divinization.

✦ Meditate, especially in the form of divine reading (see chapter 4, "How to Listen to the Readings"), on the book of Daniel, chapter 3.

✦ As the gifts are brought to the altar, be sure that your spiritual offering of yourself is a part of them.

✦ See your prayers, works, joys, and sufferings, and those of all others throughout the world, being poured into the chalice in the water and joined with the wine of Christ's offering. Consider yourself as a particular grain of wheat, a part of the larger Host of Jesus' Mystical Body.

6

How to Participate in the Eucharistic Prayer

You are a priest forever in the manner of Melchizedek.

—Psalm 110:4

Near the center of the ceiling of the Sistine Chapel in Rome, the famous image of Adam's creation at the hand of God is a majestic reminder of our humble dependency on God for our very being. The height of creative genius, this heavenly image looks down upon twenty-five thousand visitors each day, or about five million every year. Whether as faithful pilgrims or curious tourists, the chapel's guests can't help but gaze up at this work of art. What do they see? Some see color, form, and beauty; others see faith and inspiration; and still others see beauty and faith commingled in some of Michelangelo's more subtle meanings.

On the right side of the image, for example, God the Father is surrounded by a number of human and heavenly beings residing in what appears to be the shape of the human brain—Michelangelo's sixteenth-century commentary on intelligent design! The image of God the Father shows His body in a convex shape, His hand reaching toward the first man. God's posture complements

Adam's—a reflection of God, made in His image. Earthly Adam is reclining, his body mirroring his heavenly Creator's, resting in a concave shape. His left hand extends to receive the divine spark of life from the Father's right hand. Some also see in the lounging body of Michelangelo's Adam the latent Eve, her torso appearing in his bent knee. See if you can find these elements the next time you happen across the image.

Another interpretation of *The Creation of Adam* gives insight into liturgical participation, especially of the priestly sort. At the center of this central picture of the Sistine Chapel's ceiling are God's and Adam's fingers about to touch, putting the capstone on the Trinity's visible creation. But these figures are *not yet touching*, and the space between them—and the power to fill it—begins to speak directly about priesthood. The adjoining panels in the chapel's ceiling help us to see why.

The fresco next to *The Creation of Adam* depicts Eve being created out of the side of the sleeping Adam, and the one after it depicts their fall from grace at the tree and their subsequent expulsion from the garden. These panels can be given a priestly reading by those fingers about to touch. If that first contact created life, and if the continued contact sustained and developed it, then Adam's sin withdraws the human hand from God and ushers in death. Consequently, if fallen man and moaning creation wish to return to a new life, they must reach out and contact God once again. The gap—or, better, the *chasm*—must be bridged. And this is the job of the priest.

There are a few words our Roman Rite uses to describe its priests, and one of them is *pontifex*. In Latin, the noun *pons* means "bridge," and we can see this word surface in such words as "pontoon boat," which, in essence, is a small floating bridge. *Fex* is the foundation of today's "factory," the place where things are built. Put the two words together—*pontifex*—and you get "bridge builder," which is precisely what a priest is. In this job description, a priest has the power to overcome the separation between humanity and divinity, allowing men and women to pass over to heaven and unite themselves with God. In terms of Michelangelo's *Creation of Adam*, the priest bridges the gap between the outstretched fingers of God and man, a void that appeared because of sin.

Throughout history, many have noticed that things aren't quite right with the world around us and have sought either a priest or at least priestly power to commune with the divine. In fact, the priestly instinct is a part of human nature, since our constitution is perfectly suited to reconnect heaven and earth. On the one hand, we share much in common with the rest of visible creation, since we are composed in part of a material body. We love dogs and cats, flowers and trees, clouds and air, food and drink. On the other hand, we resemble invisible creation, the angels, since we possess immaterial souls. We desire to know and seek justice, we love (or at times hate) one another, and we are universally dissatisfied with the superficial happiness that material possessions bring. We look like animals but think like angels, with one foot in the earthly world and another in the heavenly world, and so we occupy a unique place in all of creation to bridge, mediate, and intercede between the opposite sides of the abyss separating us from God (see CCC 355). Some in the Church's Tradition have even called man not *Homo sapiens* (since we are often as foolish as we are sapient), but *Homo adorans*, the "worshipping man." But we are also fallen "priests of creation" and are in need of a supernatural cure for our priestly shortcomings.

A key thread throughout the Old Testament—perhaps *the* key thread—is the formation of priests. The Trinity works to restore and perfect the priesthood, both individually and collectively, a work that reaches its perfection in Jesus, the greatest bridge builder of them all, the *Pontifex Maximus*. Let's consider a few of these priests of the Old Testament and how they led the Chosen People to pass over to God.

Something of a mystery man when it comes to priests in the Bible, the figure of Melchizedek is a remarkable example of how the sacerdotal is able to bridge the gap between man and God. It should come as no surprise that Melchizedek has much in common with the Christ yet to come. First, he is not only a priest but also a king, just like Jesus, and he's not any old king either, but the royal head of Jerusalem, the place where Christ will one day offer Himself. According to the Letter to the Hebrews, Melchizedek is also "without father, mother, or ancestry, without beginning of days or end of life; thus made to resemble the Son of God, he remains a priest forever" (7:3). He also offers bread and wine, which Jesus will also do at the Last Supper. The fourth-century Doctor of the Church St. Ambrose saw in Melchizedek's offering a universal sacrifice, one given in all times and places ("from the rising of the sun to its setting," as the prophet Malachi would put it [1:11]). Melchizedek would be making an offering not bound to the future Temple of Jerusalem and its restrictive priesthood of a single tribe, the Levites. Rather, Melchizedek's priesthood reaches further than Adam's hand. In other words, this priesthood is *big*, one that calls the universe's priests—men and women—to their original place as adoring bridge builders.

Serving as another type of priest is Abraham, whom the priestly Melchizedek blesses in God's name. A different sort of priest from Melchizedek, Abraham (or, Abram, his original name) was called by God from a foreign land and promised blessings and descendants. He routinely builds altars and offers sacrifices to God (e.g., Gen. 12:7; 12:8; 13:18), and through these altars and their sacrifices made by Abraham the priest, heaven and earth one day would be rejoined. (Altars, sacrifices, and priests are always found together.) Abraham's most significant sacrifice was his only son, Isaac, who was most dear to his heart. God tells Abraham to "offer him up as a burnt offering on one of the heights that I will point out to you" (Gen. 22:2). Isaac travels to Mount Moriah on a donkey, carries the wood of his death up the mountain upon his shoulders, and freely gives himself over to his father's hands. This domestic or paternal priesthood, to be passed from father to son, was present from the start. Already naturally born priests, God's people were called upon to offer priestly sacrifice as the means to unite themselves—finger to finger—with the hand of God.

A third kind of Old Covenant priest, Moses leads his people from worldly woes to a new life. Standing at the head of his people ("in the breach" between God and the Israelites, Psalm 106:23 says), he directs the fathers of households to sacrifice an unblemished lamb to ransom their firstborn children. With the blood of the lamb marking the doorways of their homes, the Lord passes over their houses, sparing them. The next day, Moses, with staff (a type of cross) in hand, leads the Jews out of Egypt's slavery, passing through the Red Sea to freedom and new life on the opposite shore. This entire people, God says to them, "will be to me a kingdom of priests, a holy nation" (Exod. 19:6), the conduit through which heaven and earth will one day reconnect.

In all these early prefigurations of Christ's priesthood, "passing over" from one state to another and reconnecting with God is a vital element. The crossing of the Red Sea is, until the coming of Jesus, the most significant passover, where the journey from point A to point B is the result of priestly bridge building between man and God. But it is not the only example of passover. After forty years of desert wandering, for example, Joshua (in Hebrew, his name is the same as Jesus) leads the Chosen People across the Jordan on dry ground, the waters of the river piling up on both sides of them, into the promised land at Jericho (Joshua 3). Elijah also passes over the Jordan at Jericho before being taken up in the fiery chariot to God. After Elijah rolls up his mantle and strikes the water, the Jordan again parts, allowing the prophet to cross. Only then did the "fiery chariot and fiery horses" appear and "Elijah went up to heaven in a whirlwind" (2 Kings 2:11). In another example of passover, the book of Ruth relates how Naomi and Ruth, living east of the Jordan River in the land of Moab, hear that the Lord has visited His people in the land of Judah "and given them food" (1:6). Then, crossing over the Jordan, they enter Bethlehem (the name means "house of bread") and receive abundant food from Boaz—so much food, in fact, that they gathered the leftovers. (Does this account remind us of another priest from Bethlehem who gave food in abundance?) In each of these three instances—Joshua, Elijah, and Naomi and Ruth—we see bridges, passovers, and journeys from slavery and hunger in this earthly life to refreshment and new life with God. Each example recounts priestly actions of bridge building and reconnecting God and man, fingertip to fingertip.

These Old Testament priests and their mediations find fulfillment in the *Pontifex Maximus*, Jesus Christ. Like Melchizedek, the eternal Jesus offers bread and wine in Jerusalem. Like Abraham, He obediently offers His heart to the Father on the wood of the Cross. Like Moses, Jesus "stands in the breach" between

God and man and builds a bridge from earth to heaven so that we can pass over to God. His redemptive bridge building is called the "Paschal Mystery," and it includes His suffering, sacrificial death, Resurrection, and Ascension to the Father's right hand. Because Jesus' priestly Paschal Mystery is the high point of His saving work, it is naturally also at the heart of the Mass.

Our devotional journey into the heart of the Mass has taken us to the Sacred Heart of the Redeemer. His heart is, as it were, a bridge, over which we pass from earth to heaven. Consider the type of bridge builder Jesus is, and why we call Him the greatest of all. If the bridge of all human desire connects earth to heaven, rejoins man to God, Jesus is the only one who could build it, since He works perfectly for both sides of the void. He is, on the one hand, entirely God, the second Person of the Blessed Trinity. He has every authority and power to reach out from heaven to earth (much as Michelangelo depicted God striving for man on the Sistine Chapel's ceiling). On the other hand, Christ is faultlessly, wholly, and completely man. But unlike that first Adam, who withdrew his hand from the life-giving touch of God, this Second Adam does not collapse under the weight of misguided desires but wills nothing but union with God. Christ the God-man is the true High Priest who bridges the great chasm created by sin. Is there a greater bridge—or bridge builder—imaginable?

With this image of the bridge builder in mind, let us return to Mass. During the Eucharistic Prayer, this great bridge opens before us. Jesus has the power to reconnect both sides, and the material He uses is His heart, the great gift that fills the space between heaven and earth. His Cross is the altar, the location—the X that marks the spot—where His heart is placed. As a willing agent in the Paschal Mystery, His ordained priest makes the Pontifical Jesus present. But even though Jesus is the offering, the altar, and the priest in history's Paschal Mystery at Mass, He still desires our assistance. Christ the High Priest is always the principal worker in the Mass, but He calls all — the ordained *and* the baptized — to be His co-workers, salvation's cooperators, priestly collaborators.

But who is this willing accomplice in the Paschal Mystery? Ordination to the priesthood conforms a man to Christ the priest and gives him unique power to exercise Jesus' priesthood at the head of the Church. Long before ordination, that man began participating in Christ's priesthood in virtue of his baptism. In addition to removing all sin, the sacrament of baptism gives a number of saving gifts: divine life of grace, gifts of the Holy Spirit, membership in the Body of Christ, and *a share in the priesthood of Christ*. All of the sacraments help us look and act and think and be like Jesus. And since priesthood is one of Christ's characteristics, so too is it a Christian characteristic. If Christ is the *Pontifex Maximus*, then you and I and each of the baptized is a *pontifex minimus*, a "little bridge builder." Our bridge is the same one that Christ builds, a bridge to which we contribute by offering ourselves. Baptismal character empowers us — and demands of us — to exercise Christ's priesthood in ourselves.

Remember our discussion on sacrifice in chapter 5, "How to Prepare the Heart at the Offertory"? The sacrifice that God wants is our whole heart. But He won't reach out and take it against our will, nor will the priest at Mass. To get my heart to the Father, I join it to Christ's on the altar that serves as the crossroad between heaven and earth. And since Jesus is the priest who empowers me to act, I actualize His priesthood in myself. In Mass, as the preparation of the altar and the gifts concludes, the priest commands us to pray that his sacrifice and ours be acceptable to God. Assuming a priestly posture, we stand "in the breach" and say: "May the Lord accept the sacrifice at your hands for the praise and glory of his name, for our good and the good of all his holy Church." The Eucharistic Prayer that follows is the time to roll up our sleeves and usher our prayers, works, joys, and sufferings over the great bridge with Jesus. St. Leo the Great once put it like this:

> For all, regenerated in Christ ... are consecrated priests by the oil of the Holy Spirit, so that beyond the special service of our ministry as [ordained] priests, all spiritual and mature Christians know that they are ... sharers in the office of the priesthood. For ... what is more priestly than to promise the Lord a pure conscience and to offer him in love unblemished victims on the altar of one's heart?[20]

Sacrifices need priests, and priests need sacrifices. After our hearts are prepared, the Eucharistic Prayer is the moment to realize our priesthood and join ourselves to God.

As daughters and sons of Adam, we were made to praise, adore, and mediate on behalf of creation. As brothers and sisters of the Second Adam, our natural desires attain supernatural power, enabling us, with the help of Christ, to redirect a fallen world to the hand of its Maker. As priests of creation, we point to the Father, who in Christ is no farther than our fingertips. Like the snapping synapses that flash between living cells in the body, the Paschal Mystery's priestly bridge illuminates our journey's main junction: the reunion of heaven and earth.

---

[20] Leo the Great, *Sermo* 4, 1–2: PL 54, 148–149, quoted in *The Office of Readings*, vol. IV, 1549–1550.

The word "liturgy" has at its root the word "work." Bridge building is in large part the work taking place at Mass. But this labor also has its reward: much as the Chosen People's crossing over the Jordan gave them the new land's milk and honey, or as Naomi and Ruth's passage gave them Bethlehem's bread, so our own work in the Eucharistic prayer will yield food: the fruit of the tree of the Cross. We'll get a taste of this food in the next chapter.

In Brief

+ A priest is a mediator and between heaven and earth. Called *pontifex*, his role is to bridge the divide between God and man.

+ God gave the Chosen People particular priests for their reconciliation with him: Melchizedek, Abraham, and Moses. Even the people as a whole was a priestly nation, one through which all the earth would return to God.

+ Priests build bridges so that men can pass over from earthly woes to heavenly blessings.

+ Jesus' Paschal Mystery consists in His suffering, death, Resurrection, and Ascension, and this mystery wholly bridges the gap between fallen earth and eternal heaven. Jesus is the *Pontifex Maximus*.

+ In history and in the Mass, Jesus is the Priest, offering, and altar of His own saving act.

+ Even though Christ does not need our assistance in His saving work, He desires it. He thus makes us sharers in His priesthood at baptism, empowering us to offer ourselves in sacrifice with Him during the Eucharistic Prayer.

THE NEXT TIME YOU GO TO MASS

✦ See the Eucharist Prayer as the zenith of the work of bridge building, the high point on a journey to God.

✦ Recall that a priest—Jesus, the ordained priest, and you—is tasked with reconnecting heaven and earth.

✦ Consider that baptism conforms you to Jesus and His priesthood and gives you the power to offer sacrifice.

✦ Following the preparation of your heart during the offertory prayers, remember that you must join these to the sacrifice of Jesus at the priest's hands, sending them across the chasm to God the Father.

7

How to Receive Communion to the Fullest

*To the victor I will give the right to eat from the
tree of life that is in the garden of God.*

—Revelation 2:7

Any road trip requires energy. Fast-food restaurants know this, and their siren songs—the waft of cooking oil carrying the unmistakable scent of french fries—have tempted many a traveler to pass through their drive-throughs. Gas stations also gear their business to the weary wanderer, their aisles filled with every imaginable road snack. But such food, while providing a short-term carbohydrate gain is often a long-term digestive loss. Rarely is the pilgrim unequivocally satisfied after succumbing to the variety in road-trip fare. Indeed, Twinkies, beef jerky, potato chips, and caffeine- and sugar-laced drinks are nowhere to be found by the USDA on yesterday's food pyramid or today's nutrition food plate.

The famed and famished Israelite pilgrims of the Old Covenant could probably relate to the modern-day road trip. True, they passed no roadside convenience store on their desert trek—even if their stomachs growled for the apparently un-healthy cucumbers, melons, leeks, onions, and garlic of their former lives (Num. 11:5). (How the food pyramid has changed over the centuries!) They knew that crossing over the desert re-quired nourishing food and drink. God knew this too and—even if He and His people quibbled from time to time about just what was on the menu—being the good Father He is, He provided manna from heaven and water from a rock.

As the pilgrim Church on earth traveling to our final home in heaven, Catholics also know something about the neces-sity of food for the journey. Recall that, as baptized priests, all the Catholic faithful are passing over a bridge that spans fallen earth to glorious heaven. Jesus has made it less laborious—He does most of the heavy lifting in the project—but for the rest of us, suffering from the effects of original sin, it is nonetheless dangerous (for that sinful chasm is deep) and still requires effort. Here too God has provided food and drink to sustain us: the Eucharist. But unlike roadside junk food that kills the diges-tion, or even the Manna from heaven that sustained only for the short term ("Your ancestors ate the manna in the desert, but they died" [John 6:49]), the Mass's Eucharistic bread and wine is out of this world.

Many of the Mass's roads converge when it comes time for receiving Holy Communion. The Cross (as we discussed in chap-ter 2, "How to Make the Sign of the Cross") is likened to the tree of life. In the Garden of Eden stood a tree of life, one from which our first parents were free to eat; in heaven's "garden of God" stands another tree of life from which the victorious have the right to eat (Rev. 2:7); and in between rises the Cross of Jesus, whose fruit is the Eucharist—and from which the world's pilgrims must eat along the journey. Thus, the wood of the Tree of the Cross that built the heart's bridge to God in the Eucharistic Prayer presents us now with another way to participate in the divine life of Jesus.

"Active participation" in the Mass—called by the Second Vatican Council "the aim to be considered before all else"[21]—is intimately associated with the worthy reception of the Eucharist. Sixty years before the Council, Pope St. Pius X (d. 1914) first used the term "active participation" on behalf of the magisterium shortly after assuming the throne of St. Peter. On the doorstep of the First World War, Pius X sought "to restore all things in Christ" (his papal motto) by infusing the unstable world with a healthy dose of the true Christian spirit. The two emphases may seem unrelated, but where is this Christian spirit to be found? In the active and authentic participation by the faithful in the saving work of Jesus made present—and even digestible—to us today in the liturgy. "We deem it necessary," Pius X wrote, "to provide before anything else for the sanctity and dignity of the temple, in which the faithful assemble for no other object than that of acquiring this spirit from its foremost and indispensable font, which is the active participation in the most holy mysteries and in the public and solemn prayer of the Church."[22] But for Pius X, as for the fathers of the Second Vatican Council who adopted his vision, active liturgical participation had little or nothing to do with how we've come to think of it (wrongly) today: such as serving at the altar, being in the choir, or proclaiming the readings. Rather, as important as these other roles are, the pinnacle of participation, he taught, is

---

[21] Second Vatican Council, *Sacrosanctum Concilium* 14.

[22] Pius X, *Tra Le Sollecitudini*.

found in fruitful and regular reception of Holy Communion. To support his plan, in 1905 this "Pope of the Blessed Sacrament" encouraged the daily reception of Holy Communion (not at all the norm, the result of overemphasizing our sin, while not seeing its cure) and, in 1910, lowered the age of a child's First Holy Communion from around age twelve to age seven, or "about the age of discretion," so even the young could access the life-giving fruit of the tree of life.

But the Eucharist isn't a magic pill, some kind of supernatural vitamin. On the contrary, the Mass's consecrated bread and wine are the Body, Blood, Soul, and Divinity of Jesus offered to the Father in the Holy Spirit—and more. Remember all those prayers, works, joys, and sufferings; the fears, loves, sins, hopes, and thanksgivings—that is, your entire human life—that you added to the Church's gifts of bread and wine when the altar was prepared? These, along with the same sacrifices of each cell of the Mystical Body of Christ, have likewise been given to God and are returned to us transformed. It was the Great Animator, the Holy Spirit, who transformed these gifts, and even He Himself is a part of our lively reception. "He who eats it with faith," said St. Ephrem, "eats Fire and Spirit.... Take and eat this, all of you, and eat with it the Holy Spirit."[23] Charged with Jesus, on fire with the Holy Spirit, divinized by the Father, and prepared in part by the heartfelt intentions of the world, food like this can only be called "heavenly"—or as we said earlier, "out of this world." The Mass's fare is, in fact, the main course of the eternal wedding banquet of Jesus and His Bride, the Church.

---

[23] Quoted in John Paul II, encyclical letter *Ecclesia de Eucharistia* (April 17, 2003), no. 17.

But as heavenly as the Eucharist is, it can be hellish to those not ready to receive it—much as the Word of God was sweet as honey in the mouth of St. John before turning sour in his stomach (Rev. 10:10). Food and drink as powerful and substantial as the Blessed Sacrament can be received fruitfully only if we are properly disposed. Not just anyone can eat fire (as St. Ephrem says) without getting burned!

Serving as a sort of divine dietician, St. Paul was the first in the Church to advise us against eating the Body and drinking the Blood of Jesus without proper preparation. "Whoever eats the bread or drinks the cup of the Lord unworthily," he warns, "will have to answer for the body and blood of the Lord. A person should examine himself, and so eat the bread and drink the cup. For anyone who eats and drinks without discerning the body, eats and drinks judgment on himself" (1 Cor. 11:27–29). Eating and drinking judgment on oneself derails our heavenward trek, leading us back into the blind alleys of sinfulness and selfishness found by Adam and Eve. St. John Chrysostom, never afraid to speak the truth, suggested that those who receive the Eucharist properly disposed share in the new life of Jesus' Resurrection, while those who received unworthily "actively participate" in Christ's murder along with His executioners.[24] When we celebrate the solemnity of Corpus Christi, the Church sings the sequence of St. Thomas Aquinas, *Lauda Sion*, which includes these cautionary stanzas:

> Bad and good the feast are sharing,
> Of what divers dooms preparing,
> Endless death, or endless life.

---

[24] John Chrysostom, *Homily 27 on 1 Corinthians*.

> Life to these, to those damnation,
> See how like participation
> Is with unlike issues rife.

Proper disposition, then, is paramount. The Eucharistic bread and wine is the same for one who is prepared and one who is not — or, similarly, for me on one day when disposed and the next day when not. But the effects could not differ more.

If Communion on a stomach empty of the proper disposition harms us, how can we be sure we have the proper disposition? At a minimum, we are to be free from mortal sin. "To choose deliberately — that is, both knowing it and willing it — something gravely contrary to the divine law and to the ultimate end of man is to commit a mortal sin" (CCC 1874). Mortally sinful acts kill all life in the soul, withering it up like the dead chaff of a field. When it encounters the divine fire of God's love in the Eucharist, the soul cannot withstand the heat. A proper disposition for Communion includes a soul capable of Eucharistic transformation.

But being in a state of grace is only the minimum required for a fruitful encounter with Jesus. The reason Holy Communion can either save us or damn us is, in part, because of what — or whom — it contains: *Jesus, on fire with the Holy Spirit, given to us from the hands of the Father.* But the purpose of Jesus' presence in the Sacrament isn't simply so He can "remain with us always" in the tabernacle. Rather, the Eucharistic Christ desires an even greater intimacy with us, one brought about through our ingesting Him and our willingness to be changed into Him. And the ingredient (or perhaps the seasoning) necessary for healthy Eucharistic eating is a large dose of humility — the larger, the better.

The word "human" comes in part from the Latin word for "dust"—the *humus*—of which men and women are formed. The humble person knows this and is disposed to act accordingly, especially when face-to-face with God. Such a humble disposition makes or breaks the entire spiritual life. As John the Baptist says, "He must increase; I must decrease" (John 3:30). Similarly, Jesus says, "Whoever loses his life for my sake will find it" (Matt. 10:39). Fruitful Eucharistic reception consists in the willingness (and it is an act of the will) to step aside and let God fill and transform us.

Let us extend the dietary image we've used in this chapter. The maxim "You are what you eat" is supremely true of the Eucharist. St. Augustine (d. 430) hears Jesus explain the dynamic process of Eucharistic conversion this way: "I am the food of grown men; grow, and you shall feed upon me; nor shall you change me, like the food of your flesh, into yourself, but you shall be changed into me."[25] In other words, that hamburger and fries at the last exit on my earthly journey is slowly but deliberately changing into me—its cholesterol, fat, carbohydrates, proteins, sodium, what have you. The Eucharistic bread and wine of my spiritual journey, on the other hand, is gradually and steadily changing me into Jesus—but only if I am disposed and humble enough to let the transformation happen.

So again, let us return to Mass to find out how and when best to prepare for receiving this divine feast. The Mass's preparatory rites immediately prior to receiving Communion dispose us to receive the Body and Blood of the Lord in the spirit of docility, humility, and desire to be transformed into Him. The Lord's

---

[25] Augustine, *Confessions*, VII, 10, 16, quoted in Benedict XIV, *Sacramentum Caritatis* (February 22, 2007), no. 70.

Prayer, the exchange of peace, the breaking of the Eucharistic bread, and the Lamb of God each expresses in its own way how Jesus wishes to bring us from sin, evil, and selfishness to mercy, grace, and communion with Him and the Church. The invitation to Communion puts a great act of humility heard once by a Roman centurion on our lips—making our mouths water for Christ. This soldier's story ought to be a model for our Eucharistic preparation.

The story begins in Capernaum, a village on the north shore of the Sea of Galilee and the site of many of Jesus' miracles. On one occasion, Jesus enters the town and is met with the request of a Roman centurion with a suffering servant near death. The centurion asks Jesus to come and heal his servant, yet he does so in all humility. "Lord, I am not worthy to have you enter under my roof; only say the word and my servant will be healed. For I too am a person subject to authority, with soldiers subject to me. And I say to one, 'Go,' and he goes; and to another, 'Come here,' and he comes; and to my slave, 'Do this,' and he does it" (Matt. 8:8–9). A Roman centurion, as his title suggests, commanded up to one hundred Roman soldiers. He was a man of power and authority. Certainly in the eyes of the world he was more important and prestigious than a lowly Jewish carpenter—and more entitled to respect than the Jews at the time, who were subject to Roman, and therefore this centurion's, authority. The centurion's humility is all the more striking because of his high office: it was not as if he were a leprous outcast or a sinful Samaritan. In response to such humility in the face of the Lord, Jesus, "amazed," responds: "Amen, I say to you, in no one in Israel have I found such faith" (Matt. 8:10). In humility, this authoritative centurion was disposed to receive Jesus under his roof. With his example before our minds and his words in our mouths—"Lord, I am not worthy that you should enter under my roof, but only say the word and my soul shall be healed"—his humility can become ours. And his would-be guest can become ours.

Our posture for receiving Communion can also express and foster our proper disposition to receive Christ in humility. Today, both standing and kneeling are options for the recipient, even though kneeling has been the Mass's traditional posture. Standing signifies respect and readiness to act, but also independence and self-assurance. Kneeling symbolizes supplication and surrender: one is nearly incapable of acting according to his own power when kneeling, which is an appropriate attitude for divinization.

Like posture, the manner of reception also helps or hinders transformation. Receiving the Lord in the hand or directly on the tongue are the usual options in today's Mass. If receiving in the hand, do as St. Cyril recommends: "In approaching, come not with your wrists extended, or your fingers spread; but make your left hand a throne for the right, as for that which is to receive a King."[26] Over the centuries, Communion on the tongue has established itself as the normative manner for receiving Communion, since, like kneeling, it signifies the necessary humble disposition of receiving, not actively taking. Whichever option you choose, the spiritual attitude of docile transformation must accompany it—without this, the manner risks becoming meaningless.

---

[26] United States Conference of Catholic Bishops, *Norms for the Distribution and Reception of Holy Communion under Both Kinds in the Dioceses of the United States of America*, no. 41, http://www.usccb.org/prayer-and-worship/the-mass/norms-for-holy-communion-under-both-kinds/index.cfm.

But even after receiving, Communion is not over any more than the last bite on your plate signals the end of a family meal. Conversation in either case ought to ensue. In Mass, that conversation should take the form of prayer—a prayer for surrender. As St. Augustine and the Capernaum centurion teach us, an encounter with Jesus should transform our fallen selves into Christ's own heavenly image. Another powerful soldier, St. Ignatius of Loyola, became an authoritative warrior for Christ. His strength was found in humility and surrender, and his prayer, the *Suscipe* ("Receive!"), is as perfect a prayer after Communion as the centurion's was before it:

> Receive, Lord, my entire freedom. Accept the whole of my memory, my intellect, and my will. Whatever I have or possess, it was You who gave it to me; I restore it to You in full, and I surrender it completely to the guidance of Your will. Give me only love of You together with Your grace, and I am rich enough and ask for nothing more. Amen.

Learning and praying this prayer for surrender after returning to our pew after Communion will ignite in us the humble power of Jesus.

The worthy reception of Holy Communion—when we are in a state of grace and truly desire to be transformed into Jesus—is the most effective way (short of martyrdom) God gives us to attain Him. Through this "fruit of the Cross" we become what we eat. St. Athanasius famously said, "God became man so that man might become God."[27] If this is true—and it is!—we become

---

[27] Athanasius, *On the Incarnation* 54, 3.

divinized, true sons and daughters of God by the Eucharist. St. Paul encourages us: "I urge you therefore, brothers, by the mercies of God, to offer your bodies as a living sacrifice, holy and pleasing to God, your spiritual worship. Do not conform yourselves to this age but *be transformed*" (Rom. 12:1–2, emphasis added). Eucharistic transformation, first of the bread into the Body of Christ, and then of us into the Body of Christ, is the high point on our journey into the Mass.

The items on today's USDA "food plate" give energy and life to any task or trek. The Eucharistic food on the Mass's paten bestows the fire of divine life for our journey to God. But as so many Gospel stories recount, encountering God impels us to tell others about Him. In our next chapter, we'll hear how the Mass's formulas for dismissal usher us out the door and into the streets—bringing with us something important, something vital, something that will save the world.

In Brief

✦ God gives His pilgrim people food and drink for their journey to the promised land of heaven, sustenance for us to pass over Christ's priestly bridge.

✦ "Active participation" in the Mass finds its pinnacle in the worthy reception of the Eucharist. It is the best way to participate in Jesus' saving work.

✦ The Eucharist is the Body, Blood, Soul, and Divinity of Jesus as well as the fire of the Holy Spirit and the divinizing power of the Father. It also returns, transformed, the sacrifices of the entire Mystical Body of Christ.

✦ Fruitful reception of the Blessed Sacrament demands that we are at least in a state of grace, free of the deadly stain of mortal sin.

✦ Receiving the Eucharist to the fullest means having a desire to be transformed by what we eat and drink—Jesus—so that Jesus can live in us. Humility and docility are needed.

✦ The Mass's preparatory rites for Communion, when prayed attentively with body and soul, cultivate the proper disposition of humility and the desire for divinization. So too do the gestures of kneeling or standing to receive Communion, and receiving the host on the tongue or in the hand.

✦ Following Communion is a time of intimate prayer with Jesus, who wishes, in St. Augustine's words, to change us into Himself.

THE NEXT TIME YOU GO TO MASS

✦ Be free from serious sin, receiving the sacrament of Penance beforehand, if necessary.

✦ Cultivate a hunger for the Eucharist by observing the Communion fast for at least an hour before receiving the Sacrament.

✦ Know that the saving work of Jesus is made most present to us in the Eucharistic bread and wine. The worthy reception of Holy Communion is the best way to share in His saving work.

✦ Be aware that the prayers, works, joys, and sufferings that you and the other members of the Body of Christ offered during the Eucharistic Prayer are being returned to you transformed by the grace of God.

✦ Remember that you are what you eat! Hear Jesus' words to St. Augustine: "Nor shall you change me, like the food of your flesh, into yourself, but you shall be changed into me."

✦ Put yourself in the shoes of the Roman centurion, who amazed Jesus with his great faith and humility, when you say: "Lord, I am not worthy that you should enter under my roof, but only say the word and my soul shall be healed."

✦ Pray St. Ignatius's *Suscipe* prayer upon returning to your pew, a prayer of surrender and union with God—which is what Communion seeks to effect.

8

How to Respond to the Dismissal

I am the door. Whoever enters through me will be saved,
and will come in and go out and find pasture.

—John 10:9

Our devotional journey into the heart of the Mass began many chapters ago (in book time) and many minutes ago (in Mass time) at the church's door. Standing before that door, we began to see the ecclesial edifice in a new light—the light of Christ. The entrance's stairs lead us up the mountain of God and into His Temple, much as the Israelites of Jesus' own time had been led in Jerusalem. The craftsmanship and detail of light fixtures, door handles, trim work, and art tell us how significant a place the church is and how important is the divine person who lives here. We notice too that the door has men and women to minister to it, as if it were a living person. These sacramental elements combine to reveal to the mindful entrant an otherwise unseen reality, whose name is Jesus.

But one thing we don't notice about the door as we pass from outdoors to inside is the exit sign perched above the lintel. If your church has such a sign (which modern construction codes usually require on new buildings), it would, of course, be visible only as you leave the church. On the one hand, these glowing green or red industrial signs seem out of place, harsh and ugly additions to an otherwise theologically informed and beautiful building. On the other hand, such signs symbolize a real theological truth about church doors. Not only should external doors sacramentalize Jesus as the welcoming door to salvation, they also should shout to its temporary worshippers, "Get out and in the name of Christ go do some good in the world!"

When the inquisitive Catholic hears Jesus calling Himself "the door," it behooves him to keep reading, to hear just what it means to be "a door." Jesus continues: "Whoever enters through me will be saved, and will come in and go out and find pasture" (John 10:9). The first part of His teaching, "whoever enters through me will be saved, and will come in," is the scriptural basis for beginning our pilgrimage into the Mass. But it is the second part, "go out and find pasture," that launches the Mass's participants out the doors.

If you are like me, this "go out" phrase is easy to overlook. I like the idea of being welcomed by Jesus, and I am comforted with the thought of the green pastures of salvation. That Jesus, His doors, their ministers, and the Mass should demand my departure at the end — "Here's your hat, what's your hurry?" — makes my ears take note, much as the exit sign catches my eye.

The exit sign, as gaudy as it may be, really does capture the essence of what happens at the end of Mass. Like many other words we've unpacked on our journey (e.g., "creed," "pontifex," "human"), the roots of "exit" will make its meaning even more flashy. *Ex* means "out," as used in the term for an insect's suit of armor — *exoskeleton* — or as used when Scripture describes God creating "out of nothing"—*ex nihilo*. *Ite* is a verb form called the imperative, which commands action. In this case, *ite* demands that we "go." Literally, "exit" orders us to "go out"—exactly as Jesus says when He refers to himself as the door. Pope Francis, like Christ the door, calls us repeatedly to get a move on and get out into the world. About the demands of the Christian door, he says, "All of us are asked to obey [Christ's] call to go forth from our own comfort zone in order to reach all the 'peripheries' in need of the light of the gospel."[28] Although I've never seen (nor would I recommend) a revolving door at the entrance or exit of a church, it does offer a helpful image: anyone moving through its turnstile too casually will end up with an unexpected boost from the rear! It's a door that commands one to move.

The Mass's dismissal formulas form a linguistic correspondence with the church's door—even as they echo the electric word "Exit" hanging above it. When we read this sign, we understand, at its core, the command to "Go out!" In Latin, the Mass's most longstanding dismissal is *Ite, missa est*, "Go forth, the Mass is ended." The same *ite*, or "go," that shines in all its gaudiness from the exit sign now issues from the mouth of the priest or deacon at Mass's end. Even the word "Mass," or *missa*, adds more thrust to the exit. The word "Mass" is related to "missile," both words coming from a Latin verb "to throw, hurl, or send." When we hear the dismissal *Ite, missa est*, "Go forth, the Mass is ended," we should hear not an invitation to "Go and have a nice day," but a command to "Get out!"—to blast out of the church building and into the street.

---

[28] Francis, apostolic exhortation *Evangelii Gaudium* (November 24, 2013), no. 20.

The command to "get out like a missile," in fact, is such an essential part of the Eucharistic celebration that the entire celebration — from the opening Sign of the Cross to the Liturgy of the Word and the Liturgy of the Eucharist — takes its name *from its conclusion!* Were the game of basketball called "the final buzzer," or the motion picture referred to as "the closing credits," identifying this intense period of liturgical prayer as the "Mass" might not seem so remarkable. Relatedly, it is noteworthy that while the Roman Rite prescribes music and texts for the entrance of Mass, the Offertory, and at Communion, it does not propose any music for the end of Mass. It's as if the command to "Go forth, the Mass is ended," and the people's response, "Thanks be to God," are the last words the Church wants to hear before returning us to the material world. The absence of this "musical bookend" gives the Mass an unfinished feel — which is precisely the point.

The simple, direct command of the Mass's four dismissal formulas reveals the urgency of this moment in the Mass:

"Go forth, the Mass is ended."

"Go and announce the Gospel of the Lord."

"Go in peace, glorifying the Lord by your life."

"Go in peace."

Each begins with the imperative "Go," commanding us out to work in the world. Author and theologian David Fagerberg hears the Mass igniting a spiritual fire in the world. "The liturgical rites detonate an explosion," he says,

> but the radiation from these sacramental outbursts is not intended to be contained by the blast walls of the sanctuary.... The structure of the church is designed to run in a straight line from the sanctuary, through the nave, and

out the narthex: a linear structure that directs the force of the liturgical explosion onto the street.[29]

Also using the energetic language of a nuclear physicist, Pope Benedict sees similar eucharistic consequences:

> The substantial conversion of bread and wine into his body and blood introduces within creation the principle of a radical change, a sort of "nuclear fission," to use an image familiar to us today, which penetrates to the heart of all being, a change meant to set off a process which transforms reality, a process leading ultimately to the transfiguration of the entire world, to the point where God will be all in all (cf. 1 Cor. 15:28).[30]

In a more temperate vein, St. Paul simply says, "The love of Christ impels us" (2 Cor. 5:14). Whichever physical image you prefer—radiation, fission, or gravitational force—one thing is clear: Mass is not meant to leave us unchanged, nor the world unchanged; rather, it should usher in (as the Mass's ushers usher us out) a new heaven and a new earth (Rev. 21:1).

Many Gospel accounts tell of similar dramatic results following authentic encounters with Christ. After the paralyzed man was lowered through the roof and healed by Jesus, the bystanders were seized with astonishment and "they glorified God, and, struck with awe," they left saying, "We have seen incredible things today" (Luke 5:26). Following her heart-to-heart meeting with Jesus at the well, the Samaritan woman "left

---

[29] David W. Fagerberg, *Consecrating the World: On Mundane Liturgical Theology* (Kettering, OH: Angelico Press, 2016), 75–76.

[30] Benedict XVI, *Sacramentum Caritatis* 11.

her water jar and went into the town and said to the people, 'Come see a man who told me everything I have done. Could he possibly be the Messiah?' They went out of the town and came to him" (John 4:28–30). Zacchaeus the crooked tax collector welcomed Jesus into his house with joy. His neighbors grumbled about his well-known misdeeds, but having invited Mercy Himself under his roof, the tax collector experienced a conversion that he expressed in a plan of action to Jesus, saying, "Half of my possessions, Lord, I shall give to the poor, and if I have extorted anything from anyone I shall repay it four times over'" (Luke 19:8).

In a true meeting with Jesus, whether face-to-face two thousand years ago or in the Mass today, each of us has an almost irresistible desire to tell others about the encounter. Often, in fact, after Jesus had performed some miracle—healing the deaf man (Mark 7:36), cleansing the leper (Mark 1:44–45), or restoring sight to two blind men (Matt. 9:30–31)—He orders the people not to tell anyone. But they cannot help themselves: "The more he ordered them not to, the more they proclaimed it" (Mark 7:36). The same dynamic can take place in the Mass: Jesus is present and encounters us in a real and powerful way. If we meet Him with our eyes and our ears and our hearts properly disposed, then we will be energized—like a rocket—to go out and ignite the world.

Perhaps the analogies of the Mass's dismissal to missiles, explosions, and atomic detonations are out of place. All analogies, as the saying goes, are imperfect. But then again, so is the world, limping along and "looking through a glass darkly," as St. Paul says (1 Cor. 13:12, KJV). Even though Peter, James, and John may have wished to remain basking in the clear light of the Transfigured Christ atop Mount Tabor, they returned to the fallen world to continue their mission. Note how soon after they've been dismissed from Tabor that they meet, upon their descent from the mountain, the boy—convulsing, screaming, and foaming at the mouth—possessed by an evil spirit. So too those of us at Mass: the time spent in Jesus' presence energizes us to meet and address the needs of a disfigured, discordant, and distressing world amidst the spiritual war for souls. C. S. Lewis once called our world "enemy-occupied territory." He explained, "Christianity is the story of how the rightful king has landed, you might say landed in disguise, and is calling us to take part in a great campaign of sabotage."[31] Like Peter, James, and John coming down from their Transfiguration "high," our mission—why we are sent—commands us to radiate Tabor's light to all whom we encounter, enlightening for them the path to Christ and, through Him, the route to heavenly victory.

Shining this same sort of light on our earthly cares, Pope Francis speaks regularly of the Church's mission to "go out" into the world, especially to its most distant and dangerous places. There are a number of models to describe the Church: *People of God, Body of Christ, Sacrament of Salvation, Kingdom of God.* Echoing C. S. Lewis and in keeping with his emphasis on the Church's saving role in an embattled world, Pope Francis regularly employs

> the image of a field hospital to describe this "Church that goes forth"; it exists where there is combat, it is not a solid structure with all the equipment where people go to receive treatment for both small and large infirmities.

---

[31] C. S. Lewis, *Mere Christianity* (Westwood, NJ: Babour and Co., 1952), 40.

It is a mobile structure that offers first aid and immediate care, so that its soldiers do not die. It's a place for urgent care, not a place to see a specialist.[32]

"Go forth, the Mass is ended" is thus a call to arms. Each parish is mobilized under its Captain, Christ the Head, equipped with Doctors of Souls, his clergy, with "lay believers in the front lines," as Pope Pius XII put it. For the laity, we who live and work and raise families in the world during the week, the World War II pope says, "The Church is the animating principle of human society" (see CCC 899). Ours is the primary task of putting boots on the ground to sabotage the enemy's designs on human souls.

As part of our training for this mission, the Mass is a sort of spiritual boot camp. For instance, at the beginning of the Mass's Eucharistic Prayer, we learn the battle cry of "Holy, holy, holy!" from heaven's own army, the angels and saints. Saints—the holy ones—model for us how to battle in the world. Their fight is not to the death but for life. The Trinity desires to share Its essence with us to make us fully alive. Our active, intelligent, and authentic participation in God's work in the Mass is the source of divine and human life. Commenting on St. Irenaeus's formula that "the glory of God is many fully alive," Pope Benedict says that it is ultimately "the very life of man, man himself as living righteously, that is the true worship of God.... [Mass] exists in order to communicate this vision."[33]

---

[32] Pope Francis, *The Name of God Is Mercy: A Conversation with Andrea Tornielli*, trans. Oonagh Stranksy (New York: Random House, 2016), 52–53.

[33] Joseph Cardinal Ratzinger (Benedict XVI), *The Spirit of the Liturgy* (San Francisco: Ignatius Press, 2000), 18.

A model of blessedness for our own times, Pier Giorgio Frassati knew how to live life to the full and was an instrument of grace to those around him. His devotion to the Eucharist and to prayer, coupled with his sacrifices and humility, animated his faith even as his soul exuberated life. Just "getting by" wasn't enough. "To live without faith," he explained, "without a patrimony to defend, without a steady struggle for truth—that is not living, but existing." Like the early Christians who simply called themselves "the living," Frassati and all of the saints could render the Christ-life, or grace, of the Mass into their Christian lives in the world. Their journey from the Mass into the world was seamless—and sanctifying. Eternal life for the saints begins here: they don't wait for the hereafter.

An important element in embracing that eternal life is surrender. St. Ignatius's prayer for surrender allows Jesus to change us into Himself after we receive Him in the Eucharist (see chapter 7, "How to Receive the Eucharist to the Fullest"). Another soldier-turned-saint, St. Francis of Assisi, helps us to pray not only for surrender but successful service as soldiers in the world. His "Peace Prayer" has helped plant Christ's standard in the workaday world for centuries. Its intentions for practicing an active sanctity in the world offer excellent insight for meditating upon the three little yet powerful words with which the Church concludes her greatest prayer: *Ite, missa est*:

> Lord, make me an instrument of Your peace.
> Where there is hatred, let me sow love.
> Where there is injury, pardon.
> Where there is doubt, faith.
> Where there is despair, hope.
> Where there is darkness, light.
> Where there is sadness, joy.

> O Divine Master, grant that I may not so
>   much seek to be consoled as to console,
>   to be understood as to understand, to be
>   loved as to love.
> For it is in giving that we receive, in pardon-
>   ing that we are pardoned, in dying that we
>   are born to eternal life.

It's easy enough to translate *Ite, missa est* as "Go forth, the Mass is ended." The more difficult project is translating "Go forth, the Mass is ended" into action. St. Francis's prayer for love, pardon, faith, and all the other features of "the living" can be our paradigm.

Jesus calls us to "be perfect, just as your heavenly Father is perfect" (Matt. 5:48). The Mass, Jesus' perfect prayer, can produce perfect people—what the Church calls saints. Living saints go out to restore the fallen world to God. Near the end of the Bible, the Victorious Lamb announces that "The old order has passed away. . . . Behold, I make all things new" (Rev. 21:4–5). At the end of the world, these same words will issue from the heavens, for the work of Jesus will be complete. When Mass ends, the command "Go forth" reminds us that we are the hands and feet, eyes and ears, hearts and voices of Christ—and that we are sent to make all things new with divine life. Put another way, our entire devotional journey through the Mass finds its ultimate destination in sanctity—on earth as it is in heaven.

In Brief

✦ The church's doors not only welcome the faithful into the Mass, but they also usher participants back out into the world at the Mass's end.

✦ The Mass's dismissal formulas, such as "Go forth, the Mass is ended," are commands to reenter the world and sanctify it.

✦ Encountering Jesus in the Sign of the Cross, the scriptural readings, and the Eucharist should ignite within us the desire to go out and tell others of the good news of Jesus.

✦ Analogous to an army or a field hospital, the Church does battle in a fallen world to restore it to Christ. The Mass equips the baptized to be saints so that they can struggle in the world unto victory with Christ.

✦ St. Francis's "Peace Prayer" unpacks the loaded words, "Go forth, the Mass is ended," and asks for the grace for us to realize them.

THE NEXT TIME YOU GO TO MASS

✦ Recall that Jesus "the door" not only welcomes us into the start of Mass but orders us out of the church building at the end of Mass.

✦ Hear the dismissal for what it is: a command to *get out* into the world.

✦ See the Mass as the source and font, the power-house, of our Christian lives in the world—where the other 167 hours of the week take place.

✦ Think of Mass as a school (or "boot camp") of ho-liness, whose goal is to make perfect men, women, children—saints.

✦ Pray St. Francis's "Peace Prayer" slowly and med-itatively as a means to translate "Go forth, the Mass is ended" into the nitty-gritty of daily life. Think of specific, concrete ways to apply the grace of Mass in the week ahead.

9

"Take the I-90!"—Planning
the Sunday Drive of Your Life

✝

Interstate 90 runs just under 3,100 miles from Boston to Seattle and is the longest of the United States freeways to cross the country. An ambitious traveler wishing to experience each mile of this superhighway will pass through major cities such as Cleveland and Chicago, and encounter major man-made marvels such as the Ted Williams Tunnel beneath Boston Harbor or the mile-long floating bridges on Lake Washington, east of Seattle. Also guaranteed to rouse any drowsy traveler is the crossing of the famous Mississippi River and Columbia River, as well as the Great Divide at Homestake Pass, 6,329 feet high in the Rocky Mountains of Montana. History buffs will see the site of the 1876 Battle of Little Bighorn just east of I-90 in Montana and imagine the moment Wild Bill Hickok drew his "Dead Man's Hand" as he was shot and killed (also in 1876) in Deadwood, South Dakota. I-90 is not an easy trek; but as these various points of interest indicate, the storied highway is an interesting one.

Our devotional journey into the latitudes and longitudes of the Mass finds a suitable comparison to Interstate 90. At its best, the Mass offers landmark history lessons from salvation's key figures, the patriarchs, Jesus, and the saints. Human ingenuity and art convey the heritage of our Faith in chant, polyphony, poetry, mosaic, statuary, and stained glass. Nature combines with grace in the elements of water and oil, light and darkness, fire and wax. Our family of pilgrims passes through the city of man along a supernatural superhighway and ends in the City of God.

But like Interstate 90, the devotional journey can be long and arduous. It's often arid. Our brothers and sisters can annoy us along the way. The father of the family doesn't always follow the map as he ought, leading us on undesired detours. And the journey can take a long time.

To assist us on our journey into the heart of the Mass, and to make our pilgrimage as fruitful as possible, there are a number of "traveling tips" through the Mass that we ought to keep in mind for the next time we assist at this most important prayer of the Church. Implementing these key elements as part of our participation can become a trip down our own I-90—a personalized path into the heart of the Mass. We looked at eight individual moments or signposts along our journey:

1. How to enter the church building
2. How to make the Sign of the Cross
3. How to pray the Opening Prayer
4. How to listen to the readings
5. How to prepare the heart at the Offertory
6. How to participate in the Eucharistic Prayer
7. How to receive Communion to the fullest
8. How to respond to the dismissal

But how do we begin to put these all together?

First, as we set out, we must acquire the habit of looking beneath the surface of each ritual element to see the larger truth it represents. For example, when we consider the Sign of the Cross, we are introduced to the process called "mysta-gogy," where our liturgical understanding moves from what we can sense to what we cannot. But the Sign of the Cross isn't the only element of the Mass to be considered mystagogically. We should start to encounter each of the Mass's parts through mystagogical lenses. The sacramental surface of a liturgical cel-ebration is just that, a surface, and one meant to be scratched and uncovered. So too with each of our other sessions: the Collect included a lesson on silence, the Eucharistic Prayer demonstrated the meaning of priesthood, and the Dismissal taught us about the universal call to holiness. There's a parallel here to the points of interest we find on Interstate 90. A mere twenty-five miles south of I-90 near Rapid City, South Dakota, the great national landmark Mount Rushmore isn't simply a sculpture to admire but also, to more penetrating eyes, a symbol of the office of the president and model leadership. Similarly, as we climb out of the high plains, it's not enough that we admire the Rocky Mountains simply for their majestic beauty; these great natural cathedrals of rock and earth are also examples of geology and plate tectonics. Speaking to more personal motives for traveling I-90, visits to family and friends also hold signifi-cance. The annual trips to visit Grandpa Gene and Grandma Mary aren't just an opportunity to catch up on recent events but are also lessons about the importance of family. When we journey through the Mass, then, our minds and senses ought to be attuned to the spiritual and theological substance underlying each element.

Second, in our desire to participate more fully in Mass, we must know where to begin. At the risk of stating the obvious, one possibility is to begin at the beginning, taking the first of our eight elements, *entering the church building*, and building upon it until we reach the final feature, *the dismissal*. This plan has much going for it, since the Church's Mass, like the Jewish liturgies before it, leads participants progressively through its elements according to God's design. At Mount Sinai, for example, God establishes a model that is still with us today. First, God calls His people out of their slavery and to the base of His holy mountain. Second, He delivers His message, the contents of the Law, to the people through Moses. Third, the people, having heard God's word, respond with full hearts and throats: "Everything the LORD has said, we will do" (Exod. 19:8). Finally, Moses erects an altar and offers sacrifices to seal the newly drafted covenant between God and His people. Today's Mass follows this same paradigm: God calls the people together through His mouthpiece, the priest, in the Introductory Rites; He speaks His Word to the gathered assembly during the Liturgy of the Word; the people, in turn, respond, "I believe" in the Creed to what God has just revealed; and lastly the agreement is sealed on the altar in the sacrificial blood of the Lamb in the Liturgy of the Eucharist. Thus, passing through the various stages of the Mass from beginning to end, the Church's liturgy traces God's trajectory for us.

But perhaps beginning at the beginning isn't the best option for some of us. After all, in our highway tour across the top of the United States, unless you are on Interstate 90's endpoints—either Boston or Seattle—you will be starting somewhere in the middle of the route. In a similar way, another option for implementing the eight key elements of the Mass is to start from wherever you find yourself, that is, from the place or places you are most familiar with. If I am already accustomed to looking ahead to next Sunday's reading, then the method of divine reading examined in chapter 4, "How to Listen to the Readings," can serve as a foundation upon which the Mass's other elements can build.

Likewise, if a nightly examination of conscience and regular confession currently have a consistent place in my life, then the proper disposition for the fruitful reception of Holy Communion is already in train. Either option—beginning chronologically or with what is most familiar—will work. But be sure to take that proverbial first step of the journey somewhere!

For the third consideration for our "I-90" journey into the Mass, we must ask when is the best time to start. Even an intrepid traveler will be wary of the various obstacles associated with certain times of day or the year: rush-hour traffic on the Chicago Loop, tornados on the high plains in the spring, or heavy snow clogging up the passage through Montana's section of the Rocky Mountains in January. Knowing when to begin the transcontinental journey is as important as knowing where to begin. Likewise, the devotional journey into the Mass can also benefit from prudent timing. On the one hand, the time to participate fully is at the next Mass we attend. On the other hand, an event as important as a pilgrimage through the Mass needs a plan. Such a plan might best begin with the new year—either the civic new year, January 1, or the ecclesial new year, the First Sunday of Advent, at the end of November or the beginning of December. Either starting point will allow sufficient time to finish our journey at Lent, the perfect moment in the liturgical calendar, given the spiritual benefits it offers, to put to work our preparation for participation in the Mass. Lent and Easter are also times when our minds and hearts are ready to take on extra effort in the spiritual life, so Ash Wednesday is a worthy starting point. What could be a better resolution, in fact, than attaining holiness through prayerful participation in the Mass? Whether these times or others are chosen, begin with the long view and plan accordingly, avoiding the potholes of spiritual laxity, the tollbooth of bad habits that slow progress, and the road construction in personal or professional life that hinder us.

Fourth, share your spiritual I-90 itinerary with others, inviting one or more to travel along with you. A spouse or children may be the first choice for many, but friends and prayer groups, RCIA and CCD colleagues make for equally interesting and supportive companions. Practicing these methods for participating in the Mass with others fosters a sense of common mission and becomes an occasion for mutual learning and direction. Even family drives to and from the church can be opportunities to ask one another:

"What are you going to offer to the Father today?"

"What did you hear Jesus saying to you in the Gospel?"

"How will you live differently during the week ahead in light of the Dismissal?"

When traveling into the heart of the Mass, friends and family in the faith keep us accountable, on the right path, and make the reward of journey's end more enjoyable.

There are, no doubt, more insights, especially from the saints, to help us to enter into more active participation along our journey. But these four—seeing beneath the surface of the images speeding by, starting in the right spot, beginning at the best time of year, and finding others to journey with us—will begin and even guarantee a safe, successful, and saintly journey to Jesus in the Mass.

And, like the traveler drawing up a few final details on the itinerary, we ought to jot down one last point on our map before we head out on the highway. In truth, our journey will be less like a week-long drive across Interstate 90 from Boston to Seattle and more like a forty-year hike from Egypt's Goshen to Palestine's Jericho. Like many of life's skills—studying, playing sports, writing, balancing family finances—developing habits for prayerful liturgical participation comes with practice and patience. But prayerful practices come over time, and almost without notice, our whole being is shaped by the Mass into the image of Christ. Responding to the claim made by critics of the faith that Christianity has failed, Catholic writer G. K. Chesterton asserts: "The Christian ideal has not been tried and found wanting; it has been found difficult and left untried."[34] If the Church's methods for our active participation in the Mass are tried consistently and faithfully, our own journey will be found not wanting but rewarding.

Even if the journey is decidedly not the same thing as the destination, the two are unimaginable on their own. The Church calls this heavenly journey a pilgrimage; we can also call it our life—a life made all the richer and holier for participating in the Mass as the Church intends.

---

[34] G. K. Chesterton, *What's Wrong with the World* (San Francisco: Ignatius Press, 1994), 37.

Appendices

A

Summary Guide to Participation

✠

How to Enter the Church Building

The fundamental insight: Sacramental signs and symbols are filled with Jesus. More than mere mental reminders, and more effective than simple pointers that direct us elsewhere, liturgical sacraments and sacramentals unite heaven and earth in the Person of Christ.

The principal activity: As you approach the main entrance—don't go in the side door!—bear in mind that you approach Christ "the door," our access to the Father. Jesus "stands at the door and knocks" (Rev. 3:20), awaiting our entry. Let us "go within his gates, giving thanks," and "enter his courts with songs of praise" (Ps. 100:4).

How to Make the Sign of the Cross

The fundamental insight: Mystagogy leads the attentive participant from the visible sign to the invisible reality—who is ultimately Jesus—by looking to the roots of sacramental meaning in creation, culture, the Old Testament, Christ, and heaven.

The principal activity: Make the Sign of the Cross thoughtfully, for in it we recall our creation from the hands of the Trinity and, along with the entire cosmos, our re-creation today. By this Sign we are nourished with God-given grace, as from the very tree of life in nature's original garden. Like the Chosen People under Moses' outstretched arms along their way to a Promised Land, the Cross is our standard and protection. In the Sign of the Cross we configure ourselves to Jesus and His Cross. By this sign we are transported to heaven, where we eat the fruit of the tree of life in a restored Garden.

How to Pray the Opening Prayer

The fundamental insight: The Opening Prayer requires both individual contributions—the pleas of each member of the Mystical Body—and a leader to gather them and give voice to them to God the Father. The moment of silence following the priest's invitation "Let us pray" is a time to offer our intentions to and desires for God.

The principal activity: Formulate your intentions—sentiments of adoration, sorrow, thanksgiving, and petition—before Mass. When the priest says, "Let us pray," consciously bring these intentions forward so that he can offer them, along with everybody else's, to God.

How to Listen to the Readings

The fundamental insight: The Word of God is not simply texts spoken at Mass, but first and foremost is a Person, the Word of the Trinity. All liturgical words, in some way, make audible this divine Word. The Mass's Liturgy of the Word resembles history's larger economy of salvation: just as the Father conversed with the Chosen People through the prophets, so now does He continue the dialogue with His people in the Mass's readings.

The principal activity: In the days leading up to Sunday, follow the method of *lectio divina* for the Sunday Gospel: reading, reflecting, responding, contemplating, acting. At Mass, listen attentively with the ears of your heart. In the day or two following the Sunday hearing of the Word, recall the Gospel message and thank God for the fruits received.

How to Prepare the Heart at the Offertory

The fundamental insight: "Sacrifice," which is at the heart of Jesus' saving work, the Mass, and the Christian life, means giving undivided love to God the Father. Gifts and offerings that truly represent the heart of the giver are the true sacrifice desired by God. The objective of the preparation of the gifts and of the altar is to place our whole selves on the altar so that we can be joined with Jesus' whole self and given to God the Father.

The principal activity: Pray the Morning Offering throughout the week, and during the preparation of the altar and the gifts at Mass, consider slowly and thoughtfully what or whom you pray for; what you are working toward in the days to come; what has brought you recent joy; and each thing large or small that causes you pain or suffering. Be specific and genuine in these considerations, and place them on the altar along with the bread and wine.

How to Participate in the Eucharistic Prayer

The fundamental insight: A priest is a bridge builder, or *pontifex*, who bridges the divide separating man from God so that we can pass over from earth to heaven. Jesus' priestly Paschal Mystery—His suffering, death, Resurrection, and Ascension—bridges the gap between fallen earth and eternal heaven: He is the *Pontifex Maximus*. Even though Christ does not need our assistance in His saving work, He makes us sharers in His priesthood at baptism, empowering us to build the Paschal bridge with Him during the Eucharistic Prayer.

The principal activity: Recalling that baptism conforms us to Jesus and His priesthood and gives to each the power to offer sacrifice, following the preparation of your heart during the offertory prayers, remember that you must join these to the sacrifice of Jesus at the priest's hands, sending them across the chasm to God the Father.

How to Receive Communion to the Fullest

The fundamental insight: "Active participation" in the Mass finds its pinnacle in the worthy reception of the Eucharist. It is the best way to participate in Jesus' saving work. Receiving the Eucharist to its fullest requires a desire to be transformed by what we eat and drink — Jesus — so that He can live in us. Humility and docility are needed.

The principal activity: Hear Jesus' words to St. Augustine: "You shall not change me, like the food of your flesh, into yourself, but you shall be changed into me." Imitate the faithful, humble centurion when we say, "Lord, I am not worthy that you should enter under my roof, but only say the word and my soul shall be healed." Pray St. Ignatius's prayer of surrender and union with God upon returning to the pew:

> Receive, Lord, my entire freedom. Accept the whole of my memory, my intellect and my will. Whatever I have or possess, it was You who gave it to me; I restore it to You in full, and I surrender it completely to the guidance of Your will. Give me only love of You together with Your grace, and I am rich enough and ask for nothing more. Amen.

How to Respond to the Dismissal

The fundamental insight: The Mass's dismissal formulas are commands to reenter the world and sanctify it. Analogous to an army or a field hospital, the Church does battle in a fallen world to restore it to Christ. The Mass equips the baptized to be saints so that they can struggle in the world unto victory with Christ.

The principal activity: Recall that Jesus "the door" not only welcomes us in at the start of Mass but orders us out of the church building at the end of Mass. Pray St. Francis's "Peace Prayer" slowly and meditatively as a means to translate the dismissal into daily life. Think of specific, concrete ways to apply the grace of Mass in the week ahead.

> Lord, make me an instrument of Your peace. Where there is hatred, let me sow love. Where there is injury, pardon. Where there is doubt, faith. Where there is despair, hope. Where there is darkness, light. Where there is sadness, joy. O Divine Master, grant that I may not so much seek to be consoled as to console, to be understood as to understand, to be loved as to love. For it is in giving that we receive, in pardoning that we are pardoned, in dying that we are born to eternal life.

B

Glossary of Terms

✠

Active participation: Called by the Second Vatican Council "the aim to be considered before all else," it is the means by which we share in the salvific work of Jesus. The offering of oneself followed by the worthy reception of Holy Communion are the most efficacious means to participate actively in Jesus' priestly act (see chapter 7).

Creed: In Latin, *credo* means "I believe." Some suggest *credo* is made up of two smaller words: *cor* is the word for "heart," as in "coronary" or "cordially," while *do* means "I give" and is the origin of "donate." Thus, saying "I believe" is putting one's whole heart on the line for the Word of God just heard (see chapter 4).

Divine reading, or *lectio divina*: "The diligent reading of Sacred Scripture accompanied by prayer [which] brings about that intimate dialogue in which the person reading hears God who is speaking, and in praying, responds to him with trusting openness of heart." Its steps are (1) prayerful reading, (2) reflecting or meditating, (3) responding to God, (4) contemplating our communion with God in the Word, and (5) resolving to act according to His will (see chapter 4).

Lectionary: The book containing the readings for the Liturgy of the Word at Mass (see chapter 4).

Mortal sin: A deliberate choice of "something gravely contrary to the divine law and to the ultimate end of man" (CCC 1874; see chapter 7).

Mystagogical catechesis, or mystagogy: Literally, "being led into the mystery." Mystagogy leads the liturgical participant from the outward sign (e.g., door, bread) to an encounter with the inward reality, Jesus. To do so, mystagogical catechesis looks to the roots of sacramental meaning as found in (1) creation, (2) human nature, (3) the Old Testament, (4) the life of Jesus, and (5) heaven (see chapter 2).

Opening Prayer, or Collect: "Collect"—with the emphasis on the first syllable, "COL-lect"—is the traditional name for the Mass's Opening Prayer. By it, the desires of each cell of the Mystical Body are "collected" by their head, the priest, and presented to the Father in the single "I thirst" of the Mystical Body of Jesus (see chapter 3).

Paschal Mystery: Jesus' suffering, sacrificial death, Resurrection, and Ascension to the Father's right hand that reconnects earth to heaven (see chapter 6).

Pontifex: One of the Church's words for "priest." In Latin, the noun *pons* means "bridge," and the verb *fex* is "to build." Together, *pontifex* designates a "bridge builder." A priest, or *pontifex*, has the power to bridge the separation between humanity and divinity, allowing men and women to pass over from earth to heaven and unite themselves with God (see chapter 6).

Pontifex Maximus: Literally, the "Greatest Bridge Builder"—Jesus the High Priest (see chapter 6).

Prayer: Heart-to-heart communication with God. St. Augustine calls prayer "the encounter of God's thirst with ours. God thirsts that we may thirst for him" (see chapter 3).

Sacerdotal: Priestly (see chapter 6).

Sacrament: An outward sign, instituted by Christ and entrusted to His Church, by which divine life is dispensed to us by the work of the Holy Spirit (see chapter 1).

Sacramental principle: How the unseen God comes to us, and we to Him, through the medium of sensible signs (see chapter 1).

Sacrifice: Essentially joining our hearts and our whole selves through Jesus to the Father. Pope Benedict XVI describes sacrifice as "returning to love and therefore divinization" and "transformation into love" (see chapter 5).

Suscipe: Literally, "Receive!", a prayer authored by St. Ignatius of Loyola that pleads for surrender and union with God (see chapter 7).

C

Recommended Reading

────────────────── ✠ ──────────────────

Benedict XVI. Post-synodal apostolic exhortation *Sacramentum Caritatis*, "On the Eucharist as the Source and Summit of the Church's Life and Mission" (February 22, 2007).

————. Post-synodal apostolic exhortation *Verbum Domini*, "On the Word of God in the Life and Mission of the Church" (September 30, 2010).

Carstens, Chrisopher, and Douglas Martis. *Mystical Body, Mystical Voice: Encountering Christ in the Words of the Mass*. Chicago: Liturgy Training Publications, 2011.

Catechism of the Catholic Church, pt. II, "The Celebration of the Christian Mystery." Città del Vaticano Libreria Editrice Vaticana, 1994, 1997.

Corbon, Jean. *The Wellspring of Worship*. San Francisco: Ignatius Press, 2005.

Danielou, Jean. *The Bible and the Liturgy*. Notre Dame: University of Notre Dame Press, 2002.

Driscoll, Jeremy, OSB. *What Happens at Mass*. Chicago: Liturgy Training Publications, 2005.

Guardini, Romano. *The Spirit of the Liturgy*. New York: Crossroad, 1998.

Hahn, Scott. *The Supper of the Lamb.* New York: Doubleday, 1999.

John Paul II. Encyclical *Ecclesia de Eucharistia,* "On the Eucharist in Its Relationship to the Church" (April 17, 2003).

Ratzinger, Joseph Cardinal (Benedict XVI). *God Is Near Us: The Eucharist, the Heart of Life.* San Francisco: Ignatius Press, 2003.

———. *The Spirit of the Liturgy.* San Francisco: Ignatius Press, 2000.

Sarah, Cardinal Robert. *The Power of Silence: Against the Dictatorship of Noise.* San Francisco: Ignatius Press, 2017.

Sri, Edward. *A Biblical Walk through the Mass: Understanding What We Say and Do in The Liturgy.* West Chester, PA: Ascension Press, 2011.

Biographical Note

---✠---

Christopher Carstens is Director of the Office for Sacred Worship in the Diocese of La Crosse, Wisconsin, a visiting faculty member at Mundelein Seminary and the Liturgical Institute at the University of St. Mary of the Lake in Mundelein, Illinois, and editor of the *Adoremus Bulletin*. Along with Father Douglas Martis, Christopher is the co-author of *Mystical Body, Mystical Voice: Encountering Christ in the Words of the Mass* (Liturgy Training Publications). He lives in Soldiers Grove, Wisconsin, with his wife and eight children.

SPIRITUAL DIRECTION
∼ SERIES ∼

SOPHIA INSTITUTE PRESS

If this book has caused a stir in your heart to continue to pursue your relationship with God, we invite you to explore two extraordinary resources, SpiritualDirection.com and the Avila Institute for Spiritual Formation.

The readers of SpiritualDirection.com reside in almost every country of the world where hearts yearn for God. It is the world's most popular English site dedicated to authentic Catholic spirituality.

The Students of the Avila Institute for Spiritual Formation sit at the feet of the rich and deep well of the wisdom of the saints.

You can find more about the Avila Institute at
WWW.AVILA-INSTITUTE.COM.

Sophia Institute

Sophia Institute is a nonprofit institution that seeks to nurture the spiritual, moral, and cultural life of souls and to spread the Gospel of Christ in conformity with the authentic teachings of the Roman Catholic Church.

Sophia Institute Press fulfills this mission by offering translations, reprints, and new publications that afford readers a rich source of the enduring wisdom of mankind.

Sophia Institute also operates two popular online Catholic resources: CrisisMagazine.com and CatholicExchange.com.

Crisis Magazine provides insightful cultural analysis that arms readers with the arguments necessary for navigating the ideological and theological minefields of the day. *Catholic Exchange* provides world news from a Catholic perspective as well as daily devotionals and articles that will help you to grow in holiness and live a life consistent with the teachings of the Church.

In 2013, Sophia Institute launched Sophia Institute for Teachers to renew and rebuild Catholic culture through service to Catholic education. With the goal of nurturing the spiritual, moral, and cultural life of souls, and an abiding respect for the role and work of teachers, we strive to provide materials and programs that are at once enlightening to the mind and ennobling to the heart; faithful and complete, as well as useful and practical.

Sophia Institute gratefully recognizes the Solidarity Association for preserving and encouraging the growth of our apostolate over the course of many years. Without their generous and timely support, this book would not be in your hands.

www.SophiaInstitute.com
www.CatholicExchange.com
www.CrisisMagazine.com
www.SophiaInstituteforTeachers.org

Sophia Institute Press® is a registered trademark of Sophia Institute.
Sophia Institute is a tax-exempt institution as defined by the
Internal Revenue Code, Section 501(c)(3). Tax I.D. 22-2548708.